John Mead Gould

**Hints for Camping and Walking**

How to camp out

John Mead Gould

**Hints for Camping and Walking**
*How to camp out*

ISBN/EAN: 9783337423049

Printed in Europe, USA, Canada, Australia, Japan

Cover: Foto ©Lupo / pixelio.de

More available books at **www.hansebooks.com**

*Hints for Camping and Walking.*

# HOW TO CAMP OUT.

BY

JOHN M. GOULD,

AUTHOR OF HISTORY OF FIRST-TENTH-TWENTY-NINTH MAINE REGIMENT.

NEW YORK:
SCRIBNER, ARMSTRONG, & COMPANY.
1877.

# CONTENTS.

| CHAPTER | | PAGE |
|---|---|---|
| I. | Getting Ready | 9 |
| II. | Small Parties travelling afoot and camping | 14 |
| III. | Large Parties afoot with Baggage-Wagon | 25 |
| IV. | Clothing | 35 |
| V. | Stoves and Cooking-Utensils | 39 |
| VI. | Cooking | 44 |
| VII. | Marching | 50 |
| VIII. | The Camp | 60 |
| IX. | Tents, Tent Poles and Pins | 72 |
| X. | Miscellaneous.—General Advice | 90 |
| XI. | Diary | 107 |
| XII. | "How to do it," by Rev. Edward Everett Hale, &c. | 113 |
| XIII. | Hygienic Notes, by Dr. Elliott Coues, U.S.A. | 117 |

# PREFACE.

In these few pages I have tried to prepare something about camping and walking, such as I should have enjoyed reading when I was a boy; and, with this thought in my mind, I some years ago began to collect the subject-matter for a book of this kind, by jotting down all questions about camping, &c., that my young friends asked me. I have also taken pains, when I have been off on a walk, or have been camping, to notice the parties of campers and trampers that I have chanced to meet, and have made a note of their failures or success. The experiences of the pleasant days when, in my teens, I climbed the mountains of Oxford County, or sailed through Casco Bay, have added largely to the stock of notes; and finally the diaries of " the war," and the recollections of " the field," have contributed generously; so that, with quotations, and some help from other sources, a sizable volume is ready.

Although it is prepared for young men, — for students more especially, — it contains much, I trust, that will prove valuable to campers-out in general.

I am under obligations to Dr. Elliott Coues, of the United States Army, for the valuable advice contained in Chapter XIII.; and I esteem it a piece of good fortune that his excellent work ("Field Ornithology") should have been published before this effort of mine, for I hardly know where else I could have found the information with authority so unquestionable.

Prof. Edward S. Morse has increased the debt of gratitude I already owe him, by taking his precious time to draw my illustrations, and prepare them for the engraver.

Mr. J. Edward Fickett of Portland, a sailmaker, and formerly of the navy, has assisted in the chapter upon tents; and there are numbers of my young friends who will recognize the results of their experience, as they read these pages, and will please to receive my thanks for making them known to me.

PORTLAND, ME., January, 1877.

# HOW TO CAMP OUT.

# HOW TO CAMP OUT.

## CHAPTER I.

### GETTING READY.

THE hope of camping out that comes over one in early spring, the laying of plans and arranging of details, is, I sometimes think, even more enjoyable than reality itself. As there is pleasure in this, let me advise you to give a practical turn to your anticipations.

Think over and decide whether you will walk, go horseback, sail, camp out in one place, or what you will do; then learn what you can of the route you propose to go over, or the ground where you intend to camp for the season. If you think of moving through or camping in places unknown to you, it is important to learn whether you can buy provisions and get lodgings along your route. See some one, if you can, who has been where you think of going, and put down in a note-book all he tells you that is important.

Have your clothes made or mended as soon as you decide what you will need: the earlier you begin, the less you will be hurried at the last.

You will find it is a good plan, as fast as you think of a thing that you want to take, to note it on your memorandum; and, in order to avoid delay or haste, to cast your eyes over the list occasionally to see that the work of preparation is going on properly. It is a good plan to collect all of your baggage into one place as fast as it is ready; for if it is scattered you are apt to lose sight of some of it, and start without it.

As fast as you get your things ready, mark your name on them: mark every thing. You can easily cut a stencil-plate out of an old postal card, and mark with a common shoe-blacking brush such articles as tents, poles, boxes, firkins, barrels, coverings, and bags.

Some railroads will not check barrels, bags, or bundles, nor take them on passenger trains. Inquire beforehand, and send your baggage ahead if the road will not take it on your train.

Estimate the expenses of your trip, and take more money than your estimate. Carry also an abundance of small change.

Do not be in a hurry to spend money on new

inventions. Every year there is put upon the market some patent knapsack, folding stove, cooking-utensil, or camp trunk and cot combined; and there are always for sale patent knives, forks, and spoons all in one, drinking-cups, folding portfolios, and marvels of tools. Let them all alone: carry your pocket-knife, and if you can take more let it be a sheath or butcher knife and a common case-knife.

Take iron or cheap metal spoons.

Do not attempt to carry crockery or glassware upon a march.

A common tin cup is as good as any thing you can take to drink from; and you will find it best to carry it so that it can be used easily.[1]

Take nothing nice into camp, expecting to keep it so: it is almost impossible to keep things out of the dirt, dew, rain, dust, or sweat, and from being broken or bruised.

Many young men, before starting on their summer vacation, think that the barber must give their hair a "fighting-cut;" but it is not best to shave the head so closely, as it is then too much exposed to the sun, flies, and mosquitoes. A moderately short cut to the hair, however, is advisable for comfort and cleanliness.

---

[1] If your haversack-flap has a strap which buckles down upon the front, you can run the strap through the cup-handle before buckling; or you can buy a rein-hitch at the saddlery-hardware shop, and fasten it wherever most convenient to carry the cup.

If you are going to travel where you have never been before, begin early to study your map. It is of great importance, you will find, to learn all you can of the neighborhood where you are going, and to fix it in your mind.

So many things must be done at the last moment, that it is best to do what you can beforehand; but try to do nothing that may have to be undone.

Wear what you please if it be comfortable and durable: do not mind what people say. When you are camping you have a right to be independent.

If you are going on a walking-party, one of the best things you can do is to "train" a week or more before starting, by taking long walks in the open air.

Finally, leave your business in such shape that it will not call you back; and do not carry off keys, &c., which others must have; nor neglect to see the dentist about the tooth that usually aches when you most want it to keep quiet.

For convenience the following list is inserted here. It is condensed from a number of notes made for trips of all sorts, except boating and horseback-riding. It is by no means exhaustive, yet there are very many more things named than you can possibly use to advantage upon any one tour. Be careful not to be led astray by it into

## GETTING READY. 13

overloading yourself, or filling your camp with useless luggage. Be sure to remember this.

| | | |
|---|---|---|
| Ammon'd opodeldoc. | Fishing-tackle. | Paper |
| Axe (in cover). | Flour (prepared). | " collars. |
| Axle-grease. | Frying-pan. | Pens. |
| Bacon. | Guide-book. | Pepper. |
| Barometer (pocket). | Half-barrel. | Pickles. |
| Bean-pot. | Halter. | Pins. |
| Beans (in bag). | Hammer. | Portfolio. |
| Beef (dried). | Hard-bread. | Postage stamps. |
| Beeswax. | Harness (examine!). | Postal cards. |
| Bible. | Hatchet. | Rope. |
| Blacking and brush. | Haversack. | Rubber blanket. |
| Blankets. | Ink (portable bottle). | " coat. |
| Boxes. | Knives (sheath, table, | " boots. |
| Bread for lunch. | pocket and butcher.) | Sail-needle. |
| Brogans (oiled). | Lemons. | Salt. |
| Broom. | Liniment. | " fish. |
| Butter-dish and cover. | Lunch for day or two. | " pork. |
| Canned goods. | Maps. | Salve. |
| Chalk. | Matches and safe. | Saw. |
| Cheese. | Marline. | Shingles (for plates). |
| Clothes-brush. | Meal (in bag). | Shirts. |
| Cod-line. | Meal-bag (see p. 32). | Shoes and strings. |
| Coffee and pot. | Medicines. | Slippers. |
| Comb. | Milk-can. | Soap. |
| Compass. | Molasses. | Song-book. |
| Condensed milk. | Money ("change"). | Spade. |
| Cups. | Monkey-wrench. | Spoons. |
| Currycomb. | Mosquito-bar. | Stove (utensils in bags). |
| Dates. | Mustard and pot. | Sugar. |
| Dippers. | Nails. | Tea. |
| Dishes. | Neat's-foot oil. | Tents. |
| Dish-towels. | Night-shirt. | " poles. |
| Drawers. | Oatmeal. | " pins. |
| Dried fruits. | Oil-can. | Tooth-brush. |
| Dutch oven. | Opera-glass. | Towels. |
| Envelopes. | Overcoat. | Twine. |
| Figs. | Padlock and key. | Vinegar. |
| Firkin (see p. 48). | Pails. | Watch and key. |

# CHAPTER II.

### SMALL PARTIES TRAVELLING AFOOT AND CAMPING.

WE will consider separately the many ways in which a party can spend a summer vacation; and first we will start into wild and uninhabited regions, afoot, carrying on our backs blankets, a tent, frying-pan, food, and even a shot-gun and fishing-tackle. This is *very* hard work for a young man to follow daily for any length of time; and, although it sounds romantic, yet let no party of young people think they can find pleasure in it many days; for if they meet with a reverse, have much rainy weather, or lose their way, some one will almost surely be taken sick, and all sport will end.

If you have a mountain to climb, or a short trip of only a day or two, I would not discourage you from going in this way; but for any extended tour it is too severe a strain upon the physical powers of one not accustomed to similar hard work.

## AFOOT.—CAMPING OUT.

A second and more rational way, especially for small parties, is that of travelling afoot in the roads of a settled country, carrying a blanket, tent, food, and cooking-utensils; cooking your meals, and doing all the work yourselves. If you do not care to travel fast, to go far, or to spend much money, this is a fine way. But let me caution you first of all about overloading, for this is the most natural thing to do. It is the tendency of human nature to accumulate, and you will continually pick up things on your route that you will wish to take along; and it will require your best judgment to start with the least amount of luggage, and to keep from adding to it.

You have probably read that a soldier carries a musket, cartridges, blanket, overcoat, rations, and other things, weighing forty or fifty pounds. You will therefore say to yourself, "I can carry twenty." Take twenty pounds, then, and carry it around for an hour, and see how you like it. Very few young men who read this book will find it possible to *enjoy* themselves, and carry more than twenty pounds a greater distance than ten miles a day, for a week. To carry even the twenty pounds ten miles a day is hard work to many, although every summer there are parties who do their fifteen, twenty, and more miles daily, with big knapsacks on their backs; but it is neither wise, pleasant, nor healthful, to the average young man, to do this.

Let us cut down our burden to the minimum, and see how much it will be. First of all, you must take a rubber blanket or a light rubber coat,— something that will surely shed water, and keep out the dampness of the earth when slept on. You must have something of this sort, whether afoot, horseback, with a wagon, or in permanent camp.[1]

For carrying your baggage you will perhaps prefer a knapsack, though many old soldiers are not partial to that article. There are also for sale broad straps and other devices as substitutes for the knapsack. Whatever you take, be sure it has broad straps to go over your shoulders: otherwise you will be constantly annoyed from their cutting and chafing you.

You can dispense with the knapsack altogether in the same way that soldiers do,— by rolling up in your blanket whatever you have to

---

[1] A German officer tells me that his comrades in the Franco-Prussian war of 1870-1 had no rubber blankets; nor had they any shelter-tents such as our Union soldiers used in 1861-5 as a make-shift when their rubbers were lost. But this is nothing to you: German discipline compelled the soldiers to carry a big cloak which sheds water quite well, and is useful to a soldier for other purposes: but the weight and bulk condemn it for pleasure-seekers.

carry. You will need to take some pains in this, and perhaps call a comrade to assist you. Lay out the blanket flat, and roll it as tightly as possible without folding it, enclosing the other baggage [1] as you roll; then tie it in a number of places to prevent unrolling, and the shifting about of things inside; and finally tie or strap together the two ends, and throw the ring thus made over the shoulder, and wear it as you do the strap of the haversack,—diagonally across the body.

The advantages of the roll over the knapsack are important. You save the two and a half pounds weight; the roll is very much easier to the shoulder, and is easier shifted from one shoulder to the other, or taken off; and you can ease the

---

[1] In general it is better to put the shelter-tent in the roll, and to keep out the rubber blanket, for you may need the last before you camp. You can roll the rubber blanket tightly around the other roll (the cloth side out, as the rubber side is too slippery), and thus be able to take it off readily without disturbing the other things. You can also roll the rubber blanket separately, and link it to the large roll after the manner of two links of a chain.

burden a little with your hands. It feels bulky at first, but you soon become used to it. On the whole, you will probably prefer the roll to the knapsack; but if you carry much weight you will very soon condemn whatever way you carry it, and wish for a change.

A haversack is almost indispensable in all pedestrian tours. Even if you have your baggage in a wagon, it is best to wear one, or some sort of a small bag furnished with shoulder-straps, so that you can carry a lunch, writing-materials, guide-book, and such other small articles as you constantly need. You can buy a haversack at the stores where sportsmen's outfits are sold; or you can make one of enamel-cloth or rubber drilling, say eleven inches deep by nine wide, with a strap of the same material neatly doubled and sewed together, forty to forty-five inches long, and one and three-quarters inches wide. Cut the back piece about nineteen inches long, so as to allow for a flap eight inches long to fold over the top and down the front. Sew the strap on the upper corners of the back piece, having first sewed a facing inside, to prevent its tearing out the back.

### WOOLLEN BLANKET.

Next in the order of necessities is a woollen blanket, — a good stout one, rather than the light or flimsy one that you may think of taking. In almost all of the Northern States the summer nights are apt to be chilly; while in the mountainous regions, and at the seaside, they are often fairly cold. A lining of cotton drilling will perhaps make a thin blanket serviceable. This lining does not need to be quite as long nor as wide as the blanket, since the ends and edges of the blanket are used to tuck under the sleeper. One side of the lining should be sewed to the blanket, and the other side and the ends buttoned; or you may leave off the end buttons. You can thus dry it, when wet, better than if it were sewed all around. You can lay what spare clothing you have, and your day-clothes, between the lining and blanket, when the night is very cold.

In almost any event, you will want to carry a spare shirt; and in cold weather you can put this on, when you will find that a pound of shirt is as warm as two pounds of overcoat.

If you take all I advise, you will not absolutely need an overcoat, and can thus save carrying a number of pounds.

The tent question we will discuss elsewhere; but you can hardly do with less than a piece of shelter-tent. If you have a larger kind, the man who carries it must have some one to assist him in carrying his own stuff, so that the burden may be equalized.

If you take tent-poles, they will vex you sorely, and tempt you to throw them away: if you do not carry them, you will wonder when night comes why you did not take them. If your tent is not large, so that you can use light ash poles, I would at least start with them, unless the tent is a "shelter," as poles for this can be easily cut.

You will have to carry a hatchet; and the kind known as the axe-pattern hatchet is better than the shingling-hatchet for driving tent-pins. I may as well caution you here not to try to drive tent-pins with the flat side of the axe or hatchet, for it generally ends in breaking the handle, — quite an accident when away from home.

For cooking-utensils on a trip like that we are now proposing, you will do well to content yourself with a frying-pan, coffee-pot, and perhaps a tin pail; you can do wonders at cooking with these.

We will consider the matter of cooking and food elsewhere; but the main thing now is to know beforehand where you are going, and to learn if there are houses and shops on the route. Of course you must have food; but, if you have to carry three or four days' rations in your haversack, I fear that many of my young friends will fail to see the pleasure of their trip. Yet carry them if you must: do not risk starvation, whatever you do. Also remember to always have something in your haversack, no matter how easy it is to buy what you want.

I have now enumerated the principal articles of weight that a party must take on a walking-tour when they camp out, and cook as they go. If the trip is made early or late in the season, you must take more clothing. If you are gunning, your gun, &c., add still more weight. Every one will carry towel, soap, comb, and toothbrush.

Then there is a match-safe (which should be air-tight, or the matches will soon spoil), a box of salve, the knives, fork, spoon, dipper, portfolio, paper, Testament, &c. Every man also has something in particular that "he wouldn't be without for any thing."[1]

There should also be in every party a clothes-brush, mosquito-netting, strings, compass, song-book, guide-book, and maps, which should be company property.

I have supposed every one to be dressed about as usual, and have made allowance only for extra weight; viz., —

[1] I knew an officer in the army, who carried a rubber air-pillow through thick and thin, esteeming it, after his life and his rations, the greatest necessity of his existence. Another officer, when transportation was cut down, held to his camp-chair. Almost every one has his whim.

| | |
|---|---|
| Rubber blanket | 2½ pounds. |
| Stout woollen blanket and lining | 4½ " |
| Knapsack, haversack, and canteen | 4 " |
| Drawers, spare shirt, socks, and collars | 2 " |
| Half a shelter-tent, and ropes | 2 " |
| Toilet articles, stationery, and small wares, | 2 " |
| Food for one day | 3 " |
| Total | 20 pounds. |

You may be able to reduce the weight here given by taking a lighter blanket, and no knapsack or canteen; but most likely the food that you actually put in your haversack will weigh more than three pounds. You must also carry your share of the following things: —

| | |
|---|---|
| Frying-pan, coffee-pot, and pail | 3 pounds. |
| Hatchet, sheath-knife, case, and belt | 3 " |
| Company property named on last page | 3 " |

Then if you carry a heavier kind of tent than the "shelter," or carry tent-poles, you must add still more. Allow also nearly three pounds a day per man for food, if you carry more than enough for one day; and remember, that when tents, blankets, and clothes get wet, it adds about a quarter to their weight.

You see, therefore, that you have the prospect of hard work. I do not wish to discourage you from going in this way: on the contrary, there is a great deal of pleasure to be had by doing so. But the majority of men under twenty years of age will find no pleasure in carrying so much weight more than ten miles a day; and if a party of them succeed in doing so, and in attending to all of the necessary work, without being worse for it, they will be fortunate.

In conclusion, then, if you walk, and carry all your stuff, camping, and doing all your work, and cooking as you go, you should travel but few miles a day, or, better still, should have many days when you do not move your camp at all.

### OTHER WAYS OF GOING AFOOT.

It is not necessary to say much about the other ways of going afoot. If you can safely dispense with cooking and carrying food, much will be gained for travel and observation. The expenses, however, will be largely increased. If you can also dispense with camping, you ought then to be able to walk fifteen or twenty miles daily, and do a good deal of sight-seeing besides. You should be in practice, however, to do this.

You must know beforehand about your route, and whether the country is settled where you are going.

Keep in mind, when you are making plans, that it is easier for one or two to get accommodation at the farmhouses than for a larger party.

I heard once of two fellows, who, to avoid buying and carrying a tent, slept on hay-mows, usually without permission. It looks to me as if those young men were candidates for the penitentiary. If you cannot travel honorably, and without begging, I should advise you to stay at home.

# CHAPTER III.

## LARGE PARTY TRAVELLING AFOOT WITH BAGGAGE-WAGON.

WITH a horse and wagon to haul your baggage you can of course carry more. First of all take another blanket or two, a light overcoat, more spare clothing, an axe, and try to have a larger tent than the "shelter."

If the body of the wagon has high sides, it will not be a very difficult task to make a cloth cover that will shed water, and you will then have what is almost as good as a tent: you can also put things under the wagon. You must have a cover of some sort for your wagon-load while on the march, to prevent injury from showers that overtake you, and to keep out dust and mud. A tent-fly will answer for this purpose.

You want also to carry a few carriage-bolts, some nails, tacks, straps, a hand-saw, and axle-wrench or monkey-wrench. I have always found use for a sail-needle and twine; and I carry them

64511

now, even when I go for a few days, and carry all on my person.

The first drawback that appears, when you begin to plan for a horse and wagon, is the expense. You can overcome this in part by adding members to your company; but then you meet what is perhaps a still more serious difficulty, — the management of a large party.

Another inconvenience of large numbers is that each member must limit his baggage. You are apt to accumulate too great bulk for the wagon, rather than too great weight for the horse.

Where there are many there must be a captain, — some one that the others are responsible to, and who commands their respect. It is necessary that those who join such a party should understand that they ought to yield to him, whether they like it or not.

The captain should always consult the wishes of the others, and should never let selfish considerations influence him. Every day his decisions as to what the party shall do will tend to make some one dissatisfied; and although it is the duty of the dissatisfied ones to yield, yet, since submission to another's will is so hard, the captain must try to prevent any "feeling," and above all to avoid even the appearance of tyranny.

System and order become quite essential as our numbers increase, and it is well to have the members take daily turns at the several duties; and during that day the captain must hold each man to a strict performance of his special trust, and allow no shirking.

After a few days some of the party will show a willingness to accept particular burdens all of the time; and, if these burdens are the more disagreeable ones, the captain will do well to make the detail permanent.

Nothing tends to make ill feeling more than having to do another's work; and, where there are many in a party, each one is apt to leave something for others to do. The captain must be on the watch for these things, and try to prevent them. It is well for him, and for all, to know that he who has been a "good fellow" and genial companion at home may prove quite otherwise during a tour of camping. Besides this, it is hardly possible for a dozen young men to be gone a fortnight on a trip of this kind without some quarrelling; and, as this mars the sport so much, all should be careful not to give or take offence. If you are starting out on your first tour, keep this fact constantly in mind.

Perhaps I can illustrate this division of labor.

We will suppose a party of twelve with one horse and an open wagon, four tents, a stove, and other baggage. First, number the party, and assign to each the duties for the first day.

1. Captain.  Care of horse and wagon; loading and unloading wagon.
2. Jack.  Loading and unloading wagon.
3. Joe.  Captain's assistant and errand-boy; currying horse.
4. Mr. Smith.  Cooking and purchasing.
5. Sam.  Wood, water, fire, setting of table.
6. Tom.     "     "     "     "     . "
7. Mr. Jones.
8. Henry.
9. Bob.
10. Senior.
11. William.
12. Jake.

The party is thus arranged in four squads of three men each, the oldest at the heads. One half of the party is actively engaged for to-day, while the other half has little to do of a general nature, except that all must take turns in leading the horse, and marching behind the wagon. It is essential that this be done, and it is best that only the stronger members lead the horse.

To-morrow No. 7 takes No. 1's place, No. 8 takes No. 2's, and so on; and the first six have their semi-holiday.

In a few days each man will have shown a special willingness for some duty, which by common consent and the captain's approval he is permitted to take. The party then is re-organized as follows: —

1. Captain. General oversight; provider of food and provender.
2. Jack. Washing and the care of dishes.
3. Joe. (Worthless.)
4. Mr. Smith. Getting breakfast daily, and doing all of the cooking on Sunday.
5. Sam. (Gone home, sick of camping.)
6. Tom. Wood, water, fire, setting and clearing table.
7. Mr. Jones. Getting supper all alone.
8. Henry. Jack's partner. Care of food.
9. Bob. Currying horse, oiling axles, care of harness and wagon.
10. Senior. Packing wagon. Marching behind.
11. William. " " " "
12. Jake. Running errands.

The daily detail for leading the horse will have to be made, as before, from the stronger members of the party; and if any special duty arises it must still be done by volunteering, or by the captain's suggestion.

In this arrangement there is nothing to prevent one member from aiding another; in fact, where all are employed, a better feeling prevails, and, the work being done more quickly, there is more time for rest and enjoyment.

To get a horse will perhaps tax your judgment and capability as much as any thing in all your preparation ; and on this point, where you need so much good advice, I can only give you that of a general nature.

The time for camping out is when horses are in greatest demand for farming purposes ; and you will find it difficult to hire of any one except livery-stable men, whose charges are so high that you cannot afford to deal with them. You will have to hunt a long time, and in many places, before you will find your animal. It is not prudent to take a valuable horse, and I advise you not to do so unless the owner or a man *thoroughly* acquainted with horses is in the party. You may perhaps be able to hire horse, wagon, and driver; but a hired man is an objectionable feature, for, besides the expense, such a man is usually disagreeable company.

My own experience is, that it is cheaper to buy a horse outright, and to hire a harness and wagon ; and, since I am not a judge of horse-flesh, I get some friend who is, to go with me and advise. I find that I can almost always buy a horse, even when I cannot hire. Twenty to fifty dollars will bring as good an animal as I need. He may be old, broken down, spavined, wind-broken, or lame ; but if he is not sickly, or if his lameness is not from recent injury, it is not hard for him to haul a fair load ten or fifteen miles a day, when he is helped over the hard places.

So now, if you pay fifty dollars for a horse, you can expect to sell him for about twenty or twenty-five dollars, unless you were greatly cheated, or have abused your brute while on the trip, both of which errors you must be careful to avoid. It is a simple matter of arithmetic to calculate what is best for you to do ; but I hope on this horse question you may have the benefit of advice from some one who has had experience with the ways of the world. You will need it very much.

## WAGONS.

If you have the choice of wagons, take one that is made for carrying light, bulky goods, for your baggage will be of that order. One with a large body and high sides, or a covered wagon, will answer. In districts where the roads are mountainous, rough, and rocky, wagons hung on thoroughbraces appear to suit the people the best ; but you will have no serious difficulty with good steel springs if you put in rubber bumpers, and also strap the body to the axles, thus preventing the violent shutting and opening of the springs ; for you must bear in mind that the main leaf of a steel spring is apt to break by the sudden pitching upward of the wagon-body.

It has been my fortune twice to have to carry large loads in small low-sided wagons; and it proved very convenient to have two or three half-barrels to keep food and small articles in, and to roll the bedding in rolls three or four feet wide, which were packed in the wagon upon their ends. The private baggage was carried in meal-bags, and the tents in bags made expressly to hold them; we could thus load the wagon securely with but little tying.

For wagons with small and low bodies, it would be well to put a light rail fourteen to eighteen inches above the sides, and hold it there by six or eight posts resting on the floor, and confined to the sides of the body.

Drive carefully and slowly over bad places. It makes a great deal of difference whether a wheel strikes a rock with the horse going at a trot, or at a walk.

### HARNESS.

If your load is heavy, and the roads very hard, or the daily distance long, you had better have a collar for the horse: otherwise a breastplate-harness will do. In your kit of tools it is well to have a few straps, an awl, and waxed ends, against the time that something breaks. Oil the harness before you start, and carry about a pint of neat's-foot oil, which you can also use upon the men's boots. At night look out that the harness and all of your baggage are sheltered from dew and rain, rats and mice.

## ADVANTAGES AND DISADVANTAGES OF THIS MODE OF TRAVEL.

This way of travelling is peculiarly adapted to a party of different ages, rather than for one exclusively of young men. It is especially suitable where there are ladies who wish to walk and camp, or for an entire family, or for a school with its teachers. The necessity of a head to a party will hardly be recognized by young men; and, even if it is, they are still unwilling, as a general rule, to submit to unaccustomed restraint.

The way out of this difficulty is for one man to invite his comrades to join his party, and to make all the others understand, from first to last, that they are indebted to him for the privilege of going. It is then somewhat natural for the invited guests to look to their leader, and to be content with his decisions.

The best of men get into foolish dissensions when off on a jaunt, unless there is one, whose voice has authority in it, to direct the movements.

I knew a party of twenty or more that travelled in this way, and were directed by a trio composed of two gentlemen and one lady.

This arrangement proved satisfactory to all concerned.[1]

It has been assumed in all cases that some one will lead the horse, — not ride in the loaded wagon, — and that two others will go behind and not far off, to help the horse over the very difficult places, as well as to have an eye on the load, that none of it is lost off, or scrapes against the wheels. Whoever leads must be careful not to fall under the horse or wagon, nor to fall under the horse's feet, should he stumble. These are daily and hourly risks : hence no small boy should take this duty.[2]

[1] I never heard of a party exclusively of young men going on a tour of this kind, and consequently I cannot write their experiences ; but I can easily imagine their troubles, quarrels, and separation into cliques. I once went as captain of a party of ten, composed of ladies, gentlemen, and schoolboys. We walked around the White Mountains from North Conway to Jefferson and back, by way of Jackson. It cost each of us a dollar and thirty-two cents a day for sixteen days, including railroad fares to and from Portland, but excluding the cost of clothes, tents, and cooking-utensils. Another time a similar party of twelve walked from Centre Harbor, N.H., to Bethel, Me., in seventeen days, at a daily cost of a dollar and two cents, reckoning as before. In both cases, " my right there was none to dispute ; " and by borrowing a horse the first time, and selling at a loss of only five dollars the second, our expenses for the horse were small.

[2] In one of my tours around the mountains, a lad of sixteen, in attempting to hold up the horse's head as they were running down hill, was hit by the horse's fore-leg, knocked down, and run over by both wheels.

# CHAPTER IV.

### CLOTHING.

IF your means allow it, have a suit especially for the summer tour, and sufficiently in fashion to indicate that you are a traveller or camper.

### SHIRTS.

Loose woollen shirts, of dark colors and with flowing collars, will probably always be the proper thing. Avoid gaudiness and too much trimming. Large pockets, one over each breast, are "handy;" but they spoil the fit of the shirt, and are always wet from perspiration. I advise you to have the collar-binding of silesia, and fitted the same as on a cotton shirt, only looser; then have a number of woollen collars (of different styles if you choose), to button on in the same manner as a linen collar. You can thus keep your neck cool or warm, and can wash the collars, which soil so easily, without washing the whole shirt. The shirt should reach nearly to the knees, to prevent disorders in the stomach and bowels. There are many who will prefer cotton-and-wool goods to all-wool for shirts. The former do not shrink as much, nor are they as expensive, as the latter.

### DRAWERS.

If you wear drawers, better turn them inside out, so that the seams may not chafe you. They *must* be loose.

### SHOES.

You need to exercise more care in the selection of shoes than of any other article of your outfit. Tight boots put an end to all pleasure, if worn on the march; heavy boots or shoes, with enormously thick soles, will weary you; thin boots will not protect the feet sufficiently, and are liable to burst or wear out; Congress boots are apt to bind the cords of the leg, and thus make one lame; short-toed boots or shoes hurt the toes; loose ones do the same by allowing the foot to slide into the toe of the boot or shoe; low-cut shoes continually fill with dust, sand, or mud.

For summer travel, I think you can find nothing better than brogans reaching above the ankles, and fastening by laces or buttons as you prefer, but not so tight as to bind the cords of the foot. See that they bind nowhere except upon the instep. The soles should be wide, and the heels wide and low (about two and three-quarter inches wide by one inch high); have soles and heels well filled with iron nails. Be particular not to have steel nails, which slip so badly on the rocks.

Common brogans, such as are sold in every country-store, are the next best things to walk in ; but it is hard to find a pair that will fit a difficult foot, and they readily let in dust and earth.

Whatever you wear, break them in well, and oil the tops thoroughly with neat's-foot oil before you start; and see that there are no nails, either in sight or partly covered, to cut your feet.

False soles are a good thing to have if your shoes will admit them : they help in keeping the feet dry, and in drying the shoes when they are wet.

Woollen or merino stockings are usually preferable to cotton, though for some feet cotton ones are by far the best. Any darning should be done smoothly, since a bunch in the stocking is apt to bruise the skin.

### PANTALOONS.

Be sure to have the trousers loose, and made of rather heavier cloth than is usually worn at home in summer. They should be cut high in the waist to cover the stomach well, and thus prevent sickness.

The question of wearing "hip-pants," or using

suspenders, is worth some attention. The yachting-shirt by custom is worn with hip-pantaloons, and often with a belt around the waist; and this tightening appears to do no mischief to the majority of people. Some, however, find it very uncomfortable, and others are speedily attacked by pains and indigestion in consequence of having a tight waist. If you are in the habit of wearing suspenders, do not change now. If you do not like to wear them over the shirt, you can wear them over a light under-shirt, and have the suspender straps come through small holes in the dress-shirt. In that case cut the holes low enough so that the dress-shirt will fold over the top of the trousers, and give the appearance of hip-pantaloons. If you undertake to wear the suspenders next to the skin, they will gall you. A fortnight's tramping and camping will about ruin a pair of trousers: therefore it is not well to have them made of any thing very expensive.

Camping offers a fine opportunity to wear out old clothes, and to throw them away when you have done with them. You can send home by mail or express your soiled underclothes that are too good to lose or to be washed by your unskilled hands.

# CHAPTER V.

### STOVES AND COOKING-UTENSILS.

If you have a permanent camp, or if moving you have wagon-room enough, you will find a stove to be most valuable property. If your party is large it is almost a necessity.

For a permanent camp you can generally get something second-hand at a stove-dealer's or the junk-shop. For the march you will need a stove of sheet iron. About the simplest, smallest, and cheapest thing is a round-cornered box made of sheet iron, eighteen to twenty-four inches long and nine to twelve inches high. It needs no bottom: the ground will answer for that. The top, which is fixed, is a flat piece of sheet iron, with a hole near one end large enough for a pot or pan, and a hole (collar) for the funnel near the other end. It is well also to have a small hole, with a slide to open and close it with, in the end of the box near the bottom, so as to put in wood, and regulate the draught; but you can dispense with the slide by raising the stove from the ground when you want to admit fuel or air.

I have used a more elaborate article than this. It is an old sheet-iron stove that came home from the army, and has since been taken down the coast and around the mountains with parties of ten to twenty. It was almost an indispensable article with such large companies. It is a round-cornered box, twenty-one inches long by twenty wide, and thirteen inches high, with a slide in the front end to admit air and fuel. The bottom is fixed to the body; the top removes, and is fitted loosely to the body after the style of a firkin-cover, i.e., the flange, which is deep and strong, goes *outside* the stove. There are two holes on the top 5½ inches in diameter, and two 7½ inches, besides the collar for the funnel;

## STOVES AND COOKING-UTENSILS.

and these holes have covers neatly fitted. All of the cooking-utensils and the funnel can be packed inside the stove; and, if you fear it may upset on the march, you can tie the handles of the stove to those of the top piece.

A stove like this will cost about ten dollars; but it is a treasure for a large party or one where there are ladies, or those who object to having their eyes filled with smoke. The coffee-pot and tea-pot for this stove have "sunk bottoms," and hence will boil quicker by presenting more surface to the fire. You should cover the bottom of the stove with four inches or more of earth before making a fire in it.

To prevent the pots and kettles from smutting every thing they touch, each has a separate bag in which it is packed and carried.

The funnel was in five joints, each eighteen inches long, and made upon the "telescope" principle, which is objectionable on account of the smut and the jams the funnel is sure to receive. In practice we have found three lengths sufficient, but have had two elbows made; and with these we can use the stove in an old house, shed, or tent, and secure good draught.

If you have ladies in your party, or those to whom the rough side of camping-out offers few attractions, it is well to consider this stove question. Either of these here described must be handled and transported with care.

A more substantial article is the Dutch oven, now almost unknown in many of the States. It is simply a deep, bailed frying-pan with a heavy cast-iron cover that fits on and overhangs the top. By putting the oven on the coals, and making a fire on the cover, you can bake in it very well. Thousands of these were used by the army during the war, and they are still very extensively used in the South. If their weight is no objection to your plans, I should advise you to have a Dutch oven. They are not expensive if you can find one to buy. If you cannot find one for sale, see if you cannot improvise one in some way by getting a heavy cover for a deep frying-pan. It would be well to try such an improvisation at home before starting, and learn if it will bake or burn, before taking it with you.

Another substitute for a stove is one much used nowadays by camping-parties, and is suited for permanent camps. It is the top of an old cooking-stove, with a length or two of funnel. If you build a good tight fireplace underneath, it answers pretty well. The objection to it is the difficulty of making and keeping the fireplace tight, and it smokes badly when the wind is not favorable for draught. I have seen a great many of these in use, but never knew but one that did well in all weathers, and this had a fireplace nicely built of brick and mortar, and a tight iron door.

Still another article that can be used in permanent camps, or if you have a wagon, is the old-fashioned " Yankee baker," now almost unknown. You can easily find a tinman who has seen and can make one. There is not, however, very often an occasion for baking in camp, or at least most people prefer to fry, boil, or broil.

Camp-stoves are now a regular article of trade; many of them are good, and many are worthless. I cannot undertake to state here the merits or demerits of any particular kind; but before putting money into any I should try to get the advice of some practical man, and not buy any thing with hinged joints or complicated mechanism.

# CHAPTER VI.

### COOKING, AND THE CARE OF FOOD.

WHEN living in the open air the appetite is so good, and the pleasure of getting your own meals is so great, that, whatever may be cooked, it is excellent.

You will need a frying-pan and a coffee-pot, even if you are carrying all your baggage upon

your back. You can do a great deal of good cooking with these two utensils, after having had experience; and it is experience, rather than recipes and instructions, that you need. Soldiers in the field used to unsolder their tin canteens, and make two frying-pans of them; and I have seen a deep pressed-tin plate used by having two loops riveted on the edges opposite each other to run a handle through. Food fried in such plates needs careful attention and a low fire; and, as the plates themselves are somewhat delicate, they cannot be used roughly.

It is far better to carry a real frying-pan, especially if there are three or more in your party.

If you have transportation, or are going into a permanent camp, do not think of the tin article.

A coffee-pot with a bail and handle is better than one with a handle only, and a lip is better than a spout; since handles and spouts are apt to unsolder.

Young people are apt to put their pot or frying-pan on the burning wood, and it soon tips over. Also they let the pot boil over, and presently it unsolders for want of water. Few think to keep the handle so that it can be touched without burning or smutting; and hardly any young person knows that pitchy wood will give a bad flavor to any thing cooked over it on an open fire. Live coals are rather better, therefore, than the blaze of a new fire.

If your frying-pan catches fire inside, do not get frightened, but take it off instantly, and blow out the fire, or smother it with the cover or a board if you cannot blow it out.

You will do well to consult a cook-book if you wish for variety in your cooking; but some things not found in cook-books I will give you here.

Stale bread, pilot-bread, dried corn-cakes, and crumbs, soaked a few minutes in water, or better still in milk, and fried, are all quite palatable.

In frying bread, or any thing else, have the fat boiling hot before you put in the food: this prevents it from soaking fat.

### BAKED BEANS, BEEF, AND FISH.

Lumbermen bake beans deliciously in an iron pot that has a cover with a projecting rim to prevent the ashes from getting in the pot. The beans are first parboiled in one or two waters until the outside skin begins to crack. They are then put into the baking-pot, and salt pork at the rate of a pound to a quart and a half of dry beans is placed just under the surface of the beans. The rind of the pork should be gashed so that it will cut easily after baking. Two or three tablespoonfuls of molasses are put in, and a little salt, unless the pork is considerably lean. Water enough is added to cover the beans.

A hole three feet or more deep is dug in the ground, and heated for an hour by a good hot fire. The coals are then shovelled out, and the pot put in the hole, and immediately buried by throwing back the coals, and covering all with dry earth. In this condition they are left to bake all night.

On the same principle very tough beef was cooked in the army, and made tender and juicy. Alternate layers of beef, salt pork, and hard bread were put in the pot, covered with water, and baked all night in a hole full of coals.

Fish may also be cooked in the same way. It is not advisable, however, for parties less than six in number to trouble themselves to cook in this manner.

### CARE OF FOOD.

You had better *carry* butter in a tight tin or wooden box. In permanent camp you can sink it in strong brine, and it will keep some weeks. Ordinary butter will not keep sweet a long time in hot weather unless in a cool place or in brine. Hence it is better to replenish your stock often, if it is possible for you to do so.

You perhaps do not need to be told that when camping or marching it is more difficult to prevent loss of food from accidents, and from want of care, than when at home. It is almost daily in danger from rain, fog, or dew, cats and dogs, and from flies or insects. If it is necessary for you to take a large quantity of any thing, instead of supplying yourself frequently, you must pay particular attention to packing, so that it shall neither be spoiled, nor spoil any thing else.

You cannot keep meats and fish fresh for many hours on a summer day; but you may preserve either over night, if you will sprinkle a little salt upon it, and place it in a wet bag of thin cloth which flies cannot go through; hang the bag in a current of air, and out of the reach of animals.

In permanent camp it is well to sink a barrel in the earth in some dry, shaded place; it will answer for a cellar in which to keep your food cool. Look out that your cellar is not flooded in a heavy shower, and that ants and other insects do not get into your food.

The lumbermen's way of carrying salt pork is good. They take a clean butter-tub with four or five gimlet-holes bored in the bottom near the chimbs. Then they pack the pork in, and cover it with coarse salt; the holes let out what little brine makes, and thus they have a dry tub. Upon the pork they place a neatly fitting "follower," with a cleat or knob for a handle, and then put in such other eatables as they choose. Pork can be kept sweet for a few weeks in this way, even in the warmest weather; and by it you avoid the continual risk of upsetting and losing the brine. Before you start, see that the cover of the firkin is neither too tight nor too loose, so that wet or dry weather may not affect it too much.

I beg you to clean and wash your dishes as soon as you have done using them, instead of leaving them till the next meal. Remember to take dishcloths and towels, unless your all is a frying-pan and coffee-pot that you are carrying upon your back, when leaves and grass must be made to do dishcloth duty.

# CHAPTER VII.

### MARCHING.[1]

It is generally advised by medical men to avoid violent exercise immediately after eating. They are right; but I cannot advise you to rest long, or at all, after breakfast, but rather to finish what you could not do before the meal, and get off at once while it is early and cool. Do not hurry or work hard at first if you can avoid it.

On the march, rest often whether you feel tired or not; and, when resting, see that you do rest.

The most successful marching that I witnessed in the army was done by marching an hour, and resting ten minutes. You need not adhere strictly to this rule: still I would advise you to halt frequently for sight-seeing, but not to lie perfectly still more than five or ten minutes, as a reaction is apt to set in, and you will feel fatigued upon rising.

Experience has shown that a man travelling

---

[1] Some of the questions which properly belong under this heading are discussed elsewhere, and can be found by referring to the index.

with a light load, or none, will walk about three miles an hour; but you must not expect from this that you can easily walk twelve miles in four heats of three miles each with ten minutes rest between, doing it all in four and a half hours. Although it is by no means difficult, my advice is for you not to expect to walk at that rate, even through a country that you do not care to see. You may get so used to walking after a while that these long and rapid walks will not weary you; but in general you require more time, and should take it.

Do not be afraid to drink good water as often as you feel thirsty; but avoid large draughts of *cold* water when you are heated or are perspiring, and never drink enough to make yourself logy. You are apt to break these rules on the first day in the open air, and after eating highly salted food. You can often satisfy your thirst with simply rinsing the mouth. You may have read quite different advice[1] from this, which applies to those who travel far from home, and whose daily changes bring them to water materially different from that of the day before.

---

[1] This advice also differs from that generally given to soldiers; the army rule is as follows: "Drink well in the morning before starting, and nothing till the halt; keep the mouth shut; chew a straw or leaf, or keep the mouth covered with a cloth: all these prevent suffering from extreme thirst. Tying a handkerchief well wetted with salt water around the neck, allays thirst for a considerable time." — CRAGHILL'S *Pocket Companion*: Van Nostrand, N.Y.

It is well to have a lemon in the haversack or pocket: a drop or two of lemon-juice is a great help at times; but there is really nothing which will quench the thirst that comes the first few days of living in the open air. Until you become accustomed to the change, and the fever has gone down, you should try to avoid drinking in a way that may prove injurious. Base-ball players stir a little oatmeal in the water they drink while playing, and it is said they receive a healthy stimulus thereby.

Bathing is not recommended while upon the march. if one is fatigued or has much farther to go. This seems to be good counsel, but I do advise a good scrubbing near the close of the day; and most people will get relief by frequently washing the face, hands, neck, arms, and breast, when dusty or heated, although this is one of the things we used to hear cried down in the army as hurtful. It probably is so to some people: if it hurts you, quit it.

### FOOT-SORENESS AND CHAFING.

After you have marched one day in the sun, your face, neck, and hands will be sunburnt, your feet sore, perhaps blistered, your limbs may be chafed; and when you wake up on the morning of the second day, after an almost sleepless night, you will feel as if you had been "dragged through seven cities."

I am not aware that there is any preventive of sunburn for skins that are tender. A hat is better to wear than a cap, but you will burn under either. Oil or salve on the exposed parts, applied before marching, will prevent some of the fire; and in a few days, if you keep in the open air all the time, it will cease to be annoying.

To prevent foot-soreness, which is really the greatest bodily trouble you will have to contend with, you must have good shoes as already advised. You must wash your feet at least once a day, and oftener if they feel the need of it. The great preventive of foot-soreness is to have the feet, toes, and ankles covered with oil, or, better still, salve or mutton-tallow; these seem to act as lubricators. Soap is better than nothing. You ask if these do not soil the stockings. Most certainly they do. Hence wash your stockings often, or the insides of the shoes will become foul. Whenever you discover the slightest tendency of the feet to grow sore or to heat, put on oil, salve, or soap, immediately.

People differ as to these things. To some a salve acts as an irritant: to others soap acts in the same way. You must know before starting — your mother can tell you if you don't know yourself — how oil, glycerine, salve, and soap will affect your skin. Remember, the main thing is to keep the feet clean and lubricated. Wet feet chafe and blister more quickly than dry.

The same rule applies to chafing upon any part of the body. Wash and anoint as tenderly as possible. If you have chafed in any part on previous marches, anoint it before you begin this.

When the soldiers found their pantaloons were chafing them, they would tie their handkerchiefs around their pantaloons, over the place affected, thus preventing friction, and stopping the evil; but this is not advisable for a permanent preventive. A bandage of cotton or linen over the injured part will serve the purpose better.

Another habit of the soldiers was that of tucking the bottom of the pantaloons into their stocking-legs when it was dusty or muddy, or when they were cold. This is something worth remembering. You will hardly walk a week without having occasion to try it.

Leather leggins, such as we read about in connection with Alpine travel, are recommended by those who have used them as good for all sorts of pedestrianism. They have not come into use much as yet in America.

The second day is usually the most fatiguing. As before stated, you suffer from loss of sleep (for few people can sleep much the first night in camp), you ache from unaccustomed work, smart from sunburn, and perhaps your stomach has gotten out of order. For these reasons, when one can choose his time, it is well to start on Friday, and so have Sunday come as a day of rest and healing; but this is not at all a necessity. If you do not try to do too much the first few days, it is likely that you will feel better on the third night than at any previous time.

I have just said that your stomach is liable to become disordered. You will be apt to have a great thirst and not much appetite the first and second days, followed by costiveness, lame stomach, and a feeling of weakness or exhaustion. As a preventive, eat laxative foods on those days, — figs are especially good, — and try not to work too hard. You should lay your plans so as not to have much to do nor far to go at first. Do not dose with medicines, nor take alcoholic stimulants. Physic and alcohol may give a temporary relief, but they will leave you in bad condition. And here let me say that there is little or no need of spirits in your party. You will find coffee or tea far better than alcohol.

Avoid all nonsensical waste of strength, and gymnastic feats, before and during the march; play no jokes upon your comrades, that will make their day's work more burdensome. Young people are very apt to forget these things.

Let each comrade finish his morning nap. A

man cannot dispense with sleep, and it is cruel to rob a friend of what is almost his life and health. But, if any one of your party requires more sleep than the others, he ought to contrive to "turn in" earlier, and so rise with the company.

You have already been advised to take all the rest you can at the halts. Unsling the knapsack, or take off your pack (unless you lie down upon it), and make yourself as comfortable as you can. Avoid sitting in a draught of air, or wherever it chills you.

If you feel on the second morning as if you could never reach your journey's end, start off easily, and you will limber up after a while.

The great trouble with young people is, that they are ashamed to own their fatigue, and will not do any thing that looks like a confession. But these rules about resting, and "taking it easy," are the same in principle as those by which a horse is driven on a long journey; and it seems reasonable that young men should be favored as much as horses.

Try to be civil and gentlemanly to every one. You will find many who wish to make money out of you, especially around the summer hotels and boarding-houses. Avoid them if you can. Make your prices, where possible, before you engage.

Do not be saucy to the farmers, nor treat them

as "country greenhorns." There is not a class of people in the country of more importance to you in your travels; and you are in honor bound to be respectful to them. Avoid stealing their apples, or disturbing any thing; and when you wish to camp near a house, or on cultivated land, obtain permission from the owner, and do not make any unreasonable request, such as asking to camp in a man's front-yard, or to make a fire in dry grass or within a hundred yards of his buildings. Do not ask him to wait on you without offering to pay him. Most farmers object to having people sleep on their hay-mows; and all who permit it will insist upon the rule, "No smoking allowed here." When you break camp in the morning, be sure to put out the fires wherever you are; and, if you have camped on cleared land, see that the fences and gates are as you found them, and do not leave a mass of rubbish behind for the farmer to clear up.

### MOUNTAIN CLIMBING.

When you climb a mountain, make up your mind for hard work, unless there is a carriage-road, or the mountain is low and of gentle ascent. If possible, make your plans so that you will not have to carry much up and down the steep parts. It is best to camp at the foot of the mountain, or a part way up, and, leaving the most of your baggage there, to take an early start next morning so as to go up and down the same day. This is not a necessity, however; but if you camp on the mountain-top you run more risk from cold, fog, (clouds), and showers, and you need a warmer camp and more clothing than down below.

Often there is no water near the top: therefore, to be on the safe side, it is best to carry a canteen. After wet weather, and early in the summer, you can often squeeze a little water from the moss that grows on mountain-tops.

It is so apt to be chilly, cloudy, or showery at the summit, that you should take a rubber blanket and some other article of clothing to put on if needed. Although a man may sometimes ascend a mountain, and stay on the top for hours, in his shirt-sleeves, it is never advisable to go so thinly clad; oftener there is need of an overcoat, while the air in the valley is uncomfortably warm.

Do not wear the extra clothing in ascending, but keep it to put on when you need it. This rule is general for all extra clothing: you will find it much better to carry than to wear it.

Remember that mountain-climbing is excessively fatiguing: hence go slowly, make short rests *very* often, eat nothing between meals, and drink sparingly.

There are few mountains that it is advisable for ladies to try to climb. Where there is a road, or the way is open and not too steep, they may attempt it; but to climb over loose rocks and through scrub-spruce for miles, is too difficult for them.

# CHAPTER VIII.

### THE CAMP.

IT pays well to take some time to find a good spot for a camp. If you are only to stop one night, it matters not so much; but even then you should camp on a dry spot near wood and water, and where your horse, if you have one, can be well cared for. Look out for rotten trees that may fall; see that a sudden rain will not drown you out; and do not put your tent near the road, as it frightens horses.

For a permanent camp a good prospect is very desirable; yet I would not sacrifice all other things to this.

If you have to carry your baggage any distance by hand, you will find it convenient to use two poles (tent-poles will serve) as a hand-barrow upon which to pile and carry your stuff.

A floor to the tent is a luxury in which some indulge when in permanent camp. It is not a necessity, of course; but, in a tent occupied by ladies or children, it adds much to their comfort to have a few boards, an old door, or something of that sort, to step on when dressing. Boards or stepping-stones at the door of the tent partly prevent your bringing mud inside.

If you are on a hillside, pitch your tent so that when you sleep, if you are to sleep on the ground, your feet will be lower than your head : you will roll all night, and perhaps roll out of the tent, if you lie across the line running down hill.

As soon as you have pitched your tent, stretch a stout line from the front pole to the back one, near the top, upon which to hang your clothes. You can tighten this line by pulling inwards the foot of one pole before tying the line, and then lifting it back.

Do not put your clothes and bedding upon the bare ground : they grow damp very quickly. See, too, that the food is where ants will not get at it.

Do not forget to take two or three candles, and replenish your stock if you burn them : they sometimes are a prime necessity. Also do not pack them where you cannot easily find them in the dark. In a permanent camp you may be tempted to use a lantern with oil, and perhaps you will like it better than candles; but, when moving about, the lantern-lamp and oil-can will give you trouble. If you have no candlestick handy, you can use your pocket-knife, putting one blade in the bottom or side of the candle, and another blade into the ground or tent-pole. You can quickly cut a candlestick out of a potato, or can drive four nails in a block of wood.

If your candles get crushed, or if you have no candles, but have grease without salt in it, you can easily make a " slut " by putting the grease in a small shallow pan or saucer with a piece of wicking or cotton rag, one end of which shall be in the grease, and the other, which you light, held out of it. This is a poor substitute for daylight, and I advise you to rise and retire early (or "*turn in*" and "*turn out*" if you prefer) : you will then have more daylight than you need.

### BEDS.

Time used in making a bed is well spent. Never let yourself be persuaded that humps and hollows are good enough for a tired man. If you cut boughs, do not let large sticks go into the bed: only put in the smaller twigs and leaves. Try your bed before you " turn in," and see if it is comfortable. In a permanent camp you ought to take time enough to keep the bed soft ; and I like best for this purpose to carry a mattress when I can, or to take a sack and fill it with straw, shavings, boughs, or what not. This makes a much better bed, and can be taken out daily to the air and sun. By this I avoid the clutter there always is inside a tent filled with boughs; and, more than all, the ground or floor does not mould in damp weather, from the accumulation of rubbish on it.

It is better to sleep off the ground if you can, especially if you are rheumatic. For this purpose build some sort of a platform ten inches or more high, that will do for a seat in daytime. You can make a sort of spring bottom affair if you can find the poles for it, and have a little ingenuity and patience; or you can more quickly drive four large stakes, and nail a framework to them, to which you can nail boards or barrel-staves.[1] All this kind of work must be strong, or you can have no rough-and-tumble sport on it. We used to see in the army sometimes, a mattress with a bottom of rubber cloth, and a top of heavy drilling, with rather more cotton quilted[2] between them than is put into a thick comforter. Such a mattress is a fine thing to carry in a wagon when you are on the march; but you can make a softer bed than this if you are in a permanent camp.

### SLEEPING.

"Turn in" early, so as to be up with the sun. You may be tempted to sleep in your clothes; but if you wish to know what luxury is, take them

---

[1] Barrel-staves will not do for a double bed.
[2] It will roll up easier if the quilting runs from side to side only.

off as you do at home, and sleep in a sheet, having first taken a bath, or at least washed the feet and limbs. Not many care to do this, particularly if the evening air is chilly; but it is a comfort of no mean order.

If you are short of bedclothes, as when on the march, you can place over you the clothes you take off (see p. 19); but in that case it is still more necessary to have a good bed underneath.

You will always do well to cover the clothes you have taken off, or they will be quite damp in the morning.

See that you have plenty of air to breathe. It is not best to have a draught of air sweeping through the tent, but let a plenty of it come in at the feet of the sleeper or top of the tent.

A hammock is a good thing to have in a permanent camp, but do not try to swing it between two tent-poles : it needs a firmer support.

Stretch a clothes-line somewhere on your camp-ground, where neither you nor your visitors will run into it in the dark.

If your camp is where many visitors will come by carriage, you will find that it will pay you for your trouble to provide a hitching-post where the horses can stand safely. Fastening to guy-lines and tent-poles is dangerous.

## SINKS.

In a permanent camp you must be careful to deposit all refuse from the kitchen and table in a hole in the ground: otherwise your camp will be infested with flies, and the air will become polluted. These sink-holes may be small, and dug every day; or large, and partly filled every day or oftener by throwing earth over the deposits. If you wish for health and comfort, do not suffer a place to exist in your camp that will toll flies to it. The sinks should be some distance from your tents, and a dry spot of land is better than a wet one. Observe the same rule in regard to all excrementitious and urinary matter. On the march you can hardly do better than follow the Mosaic law (see Deuteronomy xxiii. 12, 13).

In permanent camp, or if you propose to stay anywhere more than three days, the crumbs from the table and the kitchen refuse should be carefully looked after: to this end it is well to avoid eating in the tents where you live. Swarms of flies will be attracted by a very little food.

A spade is better, all things considered, than a shovel, either in permanent camp or on the march.

## HOW TO KEEP WARM.

When a cold and wet spell of weather overtakes you, you will inquire, "How can we keep warm?" If you are where wood is very abundant, you can build a big fire ten or fifteen feet from the tent, and the heat will strike through the cloth. This is the poorest way, and if you have only shelter-tents your case is still more forlorn. But keep the fire a-going: you *can* make green wood burn through a pelting storm, but you must have a quantity of it — say six or eight large logs on at one time. You must look out for storms, and have some wood cut beforehand. If you have a stove with you, a little ingenuity will enable you to set it up inside a tent, and run the funnel through the door. But, unless your funnel is quite long, you will have to improvise one to carry the smoke away, for the eddies around the tent will make the stove smoke occasionally beyond all endurance. Since you will need but little fire to keep you warm, you can use a funnel made of boards, barrel-staves, old spout, and the like. Old tin cans, boot-legs, birch-bark, and stout paper can be made to do service as elbows, with the assistance of turf, grass-ropes, and large leaves. But I forewarn you there is not much fun, either in rigging your stove and funnel, or in sitting by it and waiting for the storm to blow it down. Still it is best to be busy.

Another way to keep warm is to dig a trench, twelve to eighteen inches wide, and about two feet deep, running from inside to the outside of the tent. The inside end of the trench should be larger and deeper; here you build your fire. You cover the trench with flat rocks, and fill up the chinks with stones and turf; boards can be used after you have gone a few feet from the fireplace. Over the outer end, build some kind of a chimney of stones, boxes, boards, or barrels. The fireplace should not be near enough to the side of the tent to endanger it; and, the taller the chimney is, the better it will draw if you have made the trench of good width and air-tight. If you can find a sheet-iron covering for the fireplace, you will be fortunate; for the main difficulty in this heating-arrangement is to give it draught enough without letting out smoke, and this you cannot easily arrange with rocks. In digging your trench and fireplace, make them so that the rain shall not flood them.

### FIREPLACE.

If flat rocks and mud are plenty, you can perhaps build a fireplace at the door of your tent (outside, of course), and you will then have something both substantial and valuable. Fold one flap of the door as far back as you can, and build one side of the fireplace against the pole,[1] and the other side against, or nearly over to, the corner of the tent. Use large rocks for the lower tiers, and try to have all three walls perpendicular and smooth inside. When up about three feet, or as high as the flap of the tent will allow without its being scorched, put on a large log of green wood for a mantle, or use an iron bar if you have one, and go on building the chimney. Do not narrow it much: the chimney should be as high as the top of the tent, or eddies of wind will blow down occasionally, and smoke you out. Barrels or boxes will do for the top, or you can make a cob-work of split sticks well daubed with mud. All the work of the fire-place and chimney must be made air-tight by filling the chinks with stones or chips and mud. When done, fold and confine the flap of the tent against the stonework and the mantle; better tie than nail, as iron rusts the cloth. Do not cut the tent either for this or any other purpose: you will regret it if you do. Keep water handy if there is much woodwork; and do not leave your tent for a long time, nor go to sleep with a big fire blazing.

If you have to bring much water into camp, remember that two pails carry about as easily as

[1] This applies, as will be seen, only to tents having two uprights, as the wall, " A," and shelter.

a single one, provided you have a hoop between to keep them away from your legs. To prevent the water from splashing, put something inside the pail, that will float, nearly as large as the top of the pail.

## HUNTERS' CAMP.

It is not worth while to say much about those hunters' camps which are built in the woods of

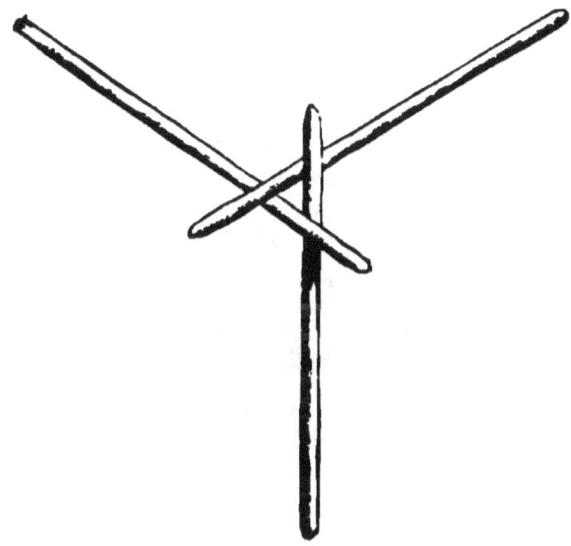

stout poles, and covered with brush or the bark of trees: they are exceedingly simple in theory, and difficult in practice unless you are accustomed to using the axe. If you go into the woods without an axeman, you had better rely upon your tents, and not try to build a camp; for when done, unless there is much labor put in it, it is not so good as a shelter-tent. You can, however, cut a few poles for rafters, and throw the shelter-tent instead of the bark or brush over the poles. You have a much larger shelter by this arrangement of the tent than when it is pitched in the regular way, and there is the additional advantage of having a large front exposed to the fire which

you will probably build; at the same time also the under side of the roof catches and reflects the heat downward. When you put up your tent in this way, however, you must look out not to scorch it, and to take especial care to prevent sparks from burning small holes in it. In fact, whenever you have a roaring fire you must guard against mischief from it.

Do not leave your clothes or blanket hanging near a brisk fire to dry, without confining them so that sudden gusts of wind shall not take them into the flame.

You may some time have occasion to make a shelter on a ledge or floor where you cannot drive a pin or nail. If you can get rails, poles, joists, or

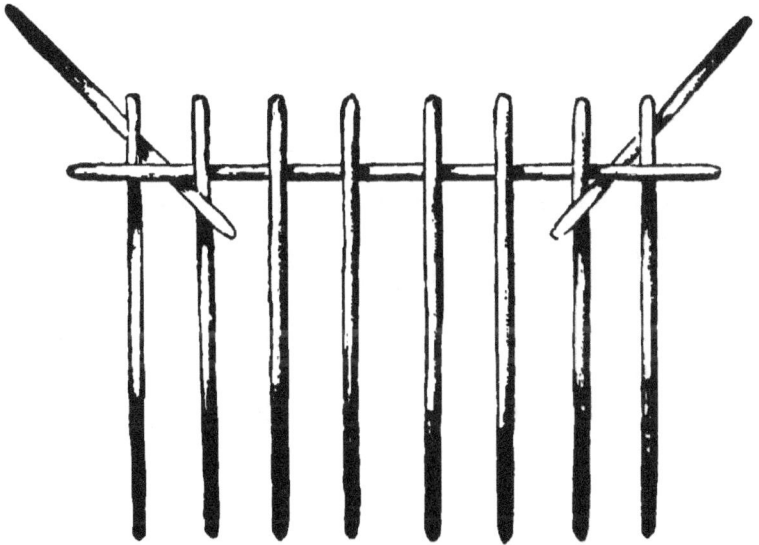

boards, you can make a frame in some one of the ways figured here, and throw your tents over it.

These frames will be found useful for other purposes, and it is well to remember how to make them.

# CHAPTER IX.

TENTS. — ARMY SHELTER-TENT (*tente d'abri*).

THE shelter-tent used by the Union soldiers during the Rebellion was made of light duck[1] about 31½ inches wide. A tent was made in two pieces both precisely alike, and each of them five feet long and five feet and two inches wide; i.e., two widths of duck. One of these pieces or half-tents was given to every soldier. That edge of the piece which was the bottom of the tent was faced at the corners with a piece of stouter duck three or four inches square. The seam in the middle of the piece was also faced at the bottom, and eyelets were worked at these three places, through which stout cords or ropes could be run to tie this side of the tent down to the tent-pin, or to fasten it to whatever else was handy. Along the other three edges of each piece of tent, at intervals of about eight inches,

---

[1] You cannot find this sort of duck in the market now, but "heavy drilling" 29½ inches wide is nearly as strong, and will make a good tent.

were button-holes and buttons; the holes an inch, and the buttons four inches, from the selvage or hem.¹

Two men could button their pieces at the tops, and thus make a tent entirely open at both ends, five feet and two inches long, by six to seven feet wide according to the angle of the roof. A third man could button his piece across one of the open ends so as to close it, although it did not make a very neat fit, and half of the cloth was not used; four men could unite their two tents by buttoning the ends together, thus doubling the length of the tent; and a fifth man could put in an end-piece.

Light poles made in two pieces, and fastened together with ferrules so as to resemble a piece of fishing-rod, were given to some of the troops when the tents were first introduced into the army; but, nice as they were at the end of the march, few soldiers would carry them, nor will you many days.

The tents were also pitched by throwing them over a tightened rope; but it was easier to *cut* a stiff pole than to *carry* either the pole or rope.

You need not confine yourself exactly to the dimensions of the army shelter-tent, but for a

---

[1] Tents made of heavy drilling were also furnished to the troops, the dimensions of which varied a trifle from those here given: they had the disadvantage of two seams instead of one.

pedestrian something of the sort is necessary if he will camp out. I have never seen a "shelter" made of *three* breadths of drilling (seven feet three inches long), but I should think it would be a good thing for four or five men to take.[1] And I should recommend that they make three-sided end-pieces instead of taking additional half-tents complete, for in the latter case one-half of the cloth is useless.

Five feet is *long* enough for a tent made on the "shelter" principle; when pitched with the roof at a right angle it is 3½ feet high, and nearly seven feet wide on the ground.

Although a shelter-tent is a poor substitute for a house, it is as good a protection as you can well carry if you propose to walk any distance. It should be pitched neatly, or it will leak. In

---

[1] If the party is of four, or even five, a shelter-tent made of three breadths of heavy drilling will accommodate all. *Sew* one end-piece to each half-tent, since sewing is better than buttoning, and the last is not necessary when your party will always camp together. Along the loose border of the end-piece work the button-holes, and sew the corresponding buttons upon the main tent an inch or more from the edge of the border. Sew on facings at the corners and seams as in the army shelter, and also on the middle of the bottom of the end-pieces; and put loops of small rope or a foot or two of stout cord through all of these facings, for the tent-pins. You will then have a tent with the least amount of labor and material in it. The top edges, like those of the army shelter, are to have buttons and button-holes; the tent can then be taken apart into two pieces, each of which will weigh about two pounds and a quarter. Nearly all of the work can be done on a sewing-machine; run two rows of stitching at each seam as near the selvage as you can.

heavy, pelting rains a fine spray will come through on the windward side. The sides should set at right angles to each other, or at a sharper angle if rain is expected.

There are rubber blankets made with eyelets along the edges so that two can be tied together to make a tent; but they are heavier, more expensive, and not much if any better; and you will need other rubber blankets to lie upon.

If you wish for a larger and more substantial covering than a "shelter," and propose to do the work yourself, you will do well to have a sailmaker or a tent-maker cut the cloth, and show you how the work is to be done. If you cannot have their help, you must at least have the assistance of one used to planning and cutting needle-work, to whom the following hints may not be lost. We will suppose heavy drilling $29\frac{1}{2}$ inches wide to be used in all instances.

### THE A-TENT.

To make an A-tent,[1] draw upon the floor a straight line seven feet long, to represent the upright pole or height of the tent; then draw a line at right angles to and across the end of the first one, to represent the ground or bottom of the tent. Complete the plan by finding where the corners will be on the ground line,

[1] Called also wedge-tent.

and drawing the two sides (roof) from the corners [1] to the top of the pole-line. This triangle is a trifle larger than the front and back of the tent will be.

The cloth should be cut so that the twilled side shall be the outside of the tent, as it sheds the rain better.

Place the cloth on the floor against the ground-line, and tack it (to hold it fast) to the pole-line, which it should overlap ⅜ of an inch; then cut by the roof-line. Turn the cloth over, and cut another piece exactly like the first; this second piece will go on the back of the tent. Now place the cloth against the ground-line as before, but upon the other side of the pole, and tack it to the floor after you have overlapped the selvage of the piece first cut ¾ of an inch. Cut by the roof-line, and turn and cut again for the back of the tent.

In cutting the four small gores for the corners, you can get all the cloth from one piece, and thus save waste, by turning and tearing it in two; these gore-pieces also overlap the longer breadths ¾ of an inch.

The three breadths that make the sides or roof are cut all alike; their length is found by

---

[1] To find the distance of the corners, multiply the width of the cloth (29¼ inches) by 3 (three breadths), and subtract 2¼ inches (or three overlappings of ¾ inch each, as will be explained).

measuring the plan from corner to corner over the top; in the plan now under consideration, the distance will be nearly sixteen feet. When you sew them, overlap the breadths ¼ of an inch the same as you do the end-breadths.

In sewing you can do no better than to run, with a machine, a row of stitching as near each selvage as possible; you will thus have two rows to each seam, which makes it strong enough. Use the coarsest cotton, No. 10 or 12.

The sides and two ends are made separately; when you sew them together care must be taken, for the edges of the ends are cut cross-grained, and will stretch very much more than the cloth of the sides (roof). About as good a seam as you can make, in sewing together the sides and ends, is to place the two edges together, and fold them outwards (or what will be downwards when the tent is pitched) twice, a quarter of an inch each time, and put two rows of stitching through if done on a machine, or one if with sail-needle and twine. This folding the cloth six-ply, besides making a good seam, strengthens the tent where the greatest strain comes. It is also advisable to put facings in the two ends of the top of the tent, to prevent the poles from pushing through and chafing.

The bottom of the tent is completed next by folding upwards and inwards two inches of cloth to make what is called a "tabling," and again folding in the raw edge about a quarter of an inch, as is usual to make a neat job. Some makers enclose a marline or other small tarred rope to strengthen the foot of the tent, and it is well to do so. One edge of what is called the "sod-cloth" is folded in with the raw edge, and stitched at the same time. This cloth, which is six to eight inches wide, runs entirely around the bottom of the tent, excepting the door-flap, and prevents a current of air from sweeping under the tent, and saves the bottom from rotting; the sod-cloth, however, will rot or wear out instead, but you can replace it much more easily than you can repair the bottom of the tent; consequently it is best to put one on.

One door is enough in an A-tent; but, if you prefer two, be sure that one at least is nicely fitted and well provided with tapes or buttons, or both: otherwise you will have a cheerless tent in windy and rainy weather. The doorflap is usually made of a strip of cloth six to nine inches wide, sewed to the selvage of the breadth that laps inside; the top of it is sewed across the inside of the other breadth, and reaches to the corner seam. Tent-makers usually determine the height of the door by having the top of the flap reach from selvage to seam as just described; the narrower the flap is, the higher the door will be. Some make the door-flap considerably wider at the bottom than at the top, and thus provide against the many annoyances that arise from one too narrow.

The loops (or "beckets" as they are called) that fasten to the tent-pins are put in one at each side of the door and at every seam. Some makers work an eyelet or put a grommet in the seam; but, in the army-tents which are made of duck, there are two eyelets worked, one on each side of the seam, and a six-thread manilla rope is run through and held in by knotting the ends.

The door is tied together by two double rows of stout tapes[1] sewed on at intervals of about eighteen inches; one inside the tent ties the door-flap to the opposite breadth, and a second set outside pulls together the two selvages of the centre breadths. Do not slight this work: a half-closed door, short tapes, and a door-flap that is slapping all the time, are things that will annoy you beyond endurance.

The upright poles of a tent such as has been described should be an inch or two more than seven feet, for the cloth will stretch. If you have a sod-cloth, the poles should be longer still.[2]

[1] What is known by shoemakers as "webbing" is good for this purpose, or you can double together and sew strips of sheeting or drilling. Cod-lines and small ropes are objectionable, as they are not easily untied when in hard knots.

[2] The poles for army A-tents are seven feet six inches.

## THE WALL-TENT.

The wall-tent is shaped like a house: the walls or sides, which are perpendicular, are four feet high. A continuous piece of cloth runs from the ground to the eaves, thence on toward the ridge-pole, and down the other side to the ground. The tent is made on the same general principles as the one last described. It is four breadths square, but the width is usually diminished about one foot by cutting six inches from each corner breadth. If the cloth is drilling or light duck, you can overlap the centre breadths a foot, and thus have the doors ready-made.

Draw a plan upon the floor as in the other case; the pole nine feet and two inches high, the corners four breadths apart less the overlappings and the narrowing; draw the wall (in the plan only) four feet and two inches high. The roof-line runs of course from the top of the pole to the top of the wall.

Cut the cloth, as before, so as to have the twilled side out. Add six inches to the distance measured on the plan, for the length of the walls and roof, so as to get cloth for the eaves.

The wall is to be four feet high; consequently, when you have sewed together the four breadths that make the roof and walls, measure four feet $3\frac{1}{2}$ inches from the ends (bottoms), double the cloth, and sew two rows of stitching by hand across from side to side, 1½ inches from the doubling; this makes the tabling for the eaves, and you have two inches left for the bottom tabling. Use stout twine for these seams at the eaves, and take only three to four stitches to the inch.

Take the same care as before in sewing together the ends and sides; the larger the tent, the more this difficulty increases.

The sod-cloth becomes more of a necessity as we increase the size of the tent, and add to the difficulty of making it fit snugly to the ground.

Facings should be put in where the ends of the poles bear, as before explained; and also in the four upper corners of the wall, to prevent the strain of the corner guy-lines from ripping apart the eaves and wall.

Beckets must be put in the bottom of each seam and the door, the same as in the A-tent, and strong tapes sewed to the door.

Guy-lines made of six-thread manilla rope are put in at the four corners of the eaves, and at every seam along that tabling, making five upon each side. Work an eyelet, or put a grommet, in the doubled cloth of the seam; knot the end of the guy-line to prevent its pulling through: tying the rope makes too bungling a job, and splicing it is too much work. The six guy-lines in the body of the tent should be about nine feet long, the four corner ones about a foot longer. The fiddles[1] should be made of some firm wood: pine and spruce will not last long enough to pay for the trouble of making them.

The poles should be nine feet and four or five inches long. If they are too long at first, sink the ends in the ground, and do not cut them off until the tent has stretched all that it will.

In permanent camp a "fly" over the tent is almost indispensable for protection from the heat and pelting rains. It should be as long as the roof of the tent, and project at least a foot beyond the eaves. The guy-lines should be a foot or more longer than those of the tent, so that the pins for the fly may be driven some distance outside those of the tent, and thus lift the fly well off the roof.

### CLOTH FOR TENTS.

For convenience we have supposed all of the tents to be made of heavy drilling. Many tent-

---

[1] This name is given to the piece of wood that tightens the guy-line. The United States army tent has a fiddle 5¼ inches long, 1¼ wide, and 1 inch thick; the holes are 3½ inches apart from centre to centre. If you make a fiddle shorter, or of thinner stock, it does not hold its gripe so well. One hole should be just large enough to admit the rope, and the other a size larger so that the rope may slide through easily.

makers consider this material sufficiently strong, and some even use it to make tents larger than the United States army wall-tent. My own experience leads me to recommend for a wall-tent a heavier cloth, known to the trade as "eight-ounce Raven's" duck,[1] because drilling becomes so thin after it has been used two or three seasons that a high wind is apt to tear it.

The cost of the cloth is about the same as the value of the labor of making the tent; but the difference between the cost of drilling and eight-ounce duck for a wall-tent of four breadths with a fly is only three to four dollars, and the duck tent will last nearly twice as long as the one of drilling. For these reasons it seems best not to put your labor into the inferior cloth.

Before you use the tent, or expose to the weather any thing made of cotton cloth, you should wash it thoroughly in strong soap-suds, and then soak it in strong brine; this takes the sizing and oil out of the cloth, and if repeated from year to year will prevent mildew, which soon spoils the cloth. There are mixtures that are said to be better still, but a tent-maker

[1] Seven-ounce duck is made, but it is not much heavier than drilling, and since it is little used it is not easily found for sale. United States army wall-tents are made from a superior quality of ten-ounce duck, but they are much stouter than is necessary for summer camping. There are also "sail-ducks," known as "No. 8," "No. 9," &c., which are very much too heavy for tents.

assures me that the yearly washing is better than any thing applied only once. Some fishermen preserve their sails by soaking them in a solution of lime and water considerably thinner than whitewash. Others soak them in a tanner's vat; but the leather-like color imparted is not pleasing to the eye. Weak lime-water they say does not injure cotton; but it ruins rope and leather, and some complain that it rots the thread.

It will save strain upon any tent, to stay it in windy weather with ropes running from the iron pins of the upright poles (which should project through the ridgepole and top of the tent) to the ground in front and rear of the tent. A still better way is to run four ropes from the top — two from each pole-pin — down to the ground near the tent-pins of the four corner guy-lines. The two stays from the rear pole should run toward the front of the tent; and the two front stays toward the rear, crossing the other two. The tent is then stayed against a wind from any quarter, and the stays and guy-lines are all together on the sides of the tent.

Loosen the stays and guy-lines a little at night or when rain is approaching, so as to prevent them from straining the tent by shrinking.

Around the bottom of any tent you should dig a small trench to catch and convey away the water when it rains; and I caution you against the error which even old campers sometimes make, — do not try to have the water run up hill.

### HOW TO PITCH A WALL-TENT QUICKLY.

After you have once pitched the tent, and have put the poles and pins in their exact places, note the distance from one of the upright poles to the pin holding one of the nearest corner guy-lines, and then mark one of the poles in such a way that you can tell by it what that distance is. When you next wish to pitch the tent, drive two small pins in the ground where the two upright poles are to rest, — the ridgepole will tell you how far apart they must be, — then, by measuring with your marked pole, you can drive the four pins for the corner guys in their proper places.

Next spread the tent on the ground, and put the ridgepole in its place in the top of the tent, and the two upright poles in their places. Then raise the tent. It will take two persons, or, if the tent is large, four or more, having first moved it bodily, to bring the feet of the upright poles to touch the two small pins that you drove at the beginning. You can now catch and tighten the corner guy-lines on the four pins previously driven. In driving the other pins, it looks well to have them on a line, if possible; also try to have the wall of the tent set square : to do this you must tie the door just right before you tighten a guy-line.

You will find this way of pitching a tent convenient when a wind is blowing, or when your assistant is not a strong person. If the wind is very high, spread your tent to windward, and catch the windward guy-lines before raising the tent. You will thus avoid having it blown over.

### TENT-POLES.

As tent-poles are not expensive, you may find it convenient to have two sets for each tent; one stout set for common use, and a lighter set to take when transportation is limited. Sound spruce, free from large knots and tolerably straight-grained, makes good poles; pine answers as well, but is more expensive.

The upright poles of a stout set for a wall-tent of the United States Army pattern should be round or eight-sided, and about two inches in diameter.[1] If you prefer to have them square, round off the edges, or they will be badly bruised upon handling. Drive a stout iron pin[2] seven or eight inches long into the centre of the top until

---

[1] The length of tent-poles, as has been previously stated, depends upon the size of the tent.

[2] What are known as "bolt-ends" can be bought at the hardware stores for this purpose.

it projects only about three and a half or four inches, or enough to go through the ridgepole and an inch beyond. It will be necessary to bore a hole in the pole before driving in the pin, to prevent splitting. A ferrule is also serviceable on this end of the pole.

The ridgepole should be well rounded on the edges, and be about two and a half inches wide and two inches thick. If made of stuff thinner than an inch and a half, it should be wider in the middle than above stated, or the pole will sag. Bore the holes to receive the pins of the uprights with an auger a size larger than the pins, so that they may go in and out easily: these holes should be an inch and a half from the ends. Ferrules or broad bands are desirable on the ends of the ridgepole; but if you cannot afford these you may perhaps be able to put a rivet or two through the pole between the ends and the holes, or, if not rivets, then screws, which are better than nothing to prevent the pin of the upright from splitting the ridge-pole.

### TENT-PINS.

Tent-pins should be made of sound hard wood; old wheel-spokes are excellent. Make them pointed at the bottom, so that they will drive easily; and notch them about two inches from the top, so that they will hold the rope. Cut away the wood from just above the notch towards the back of the head; this will prevent the notch of the pin from splitting off when it is driven. It is well to have pins differ in length and size: those for the corners and the stays should be the largest, say fifteen to eighteen inches long; and those for the wall and door may be eight or ten inches. But pins of these sizes are apt to pull out in a heavy storm; and so when you are to camp in one spot for some time, or when you see a storm brewing, it is well to make pins very stout, and two feet or more long, for the stays and four corner guy-lines, out of such stuff as you find at hand.

Loosen the pins by striking them on all four sides before you try to pull them up. A spade is a fine thing to use to pry out a pin that is deep in the ground, and a wooden mallet is better than an axe or hatchet to drive them in with; but, unless you have a large number of pins to drive, it will hardly pay you to get a mallet especially for this business.

Make a stout canvas bag to hold the tent-pins; and do not fold them loose with the tent, as it soils and wears out the cloth.

### BEST SIZE OF TENTS.

The majority of people who go into permanent camp prefer tents considerably larger than the army wall-tent; but, unless your camp is well sheltered from the wind, you will have constant and serious troubles during every gale and thunder-storm, if you are in a large or high tent. A large tent is certainly more comfortable in fine weather; but you can make a small one sufficiently cheerful, and have a sense of security in it that you cannot feel in one larger. But, if you will have a large tent, make it of something heavier than drilling.

If you have two tents of the same height, you can connect the tops with a pole, and throw a fly, blanket, or sheet over it on pleasant days.

Do not pack away a tent when it is damp if you can possibly avoid it, as it will mildew and decay in a few days of warm weather. If you are compelled to pack it when very damp, you can prevent decay by salting it liberally inside and out.

Before you put away your tent for the season be sure that it is perfectly dry, and that the dead flies and grasshoppers are swept out of the inside. You should have a stout bag to keep it in, and to prevent its being chafed and soiled when it is handled and carried. You will find a hundred good uses for the bag in camp.

# CHAPTER X.

### MISCELLANEOUS. — GENERAL ADVICE.

IF you travel horseback, singly or in parties, a previous experience in riding and in the care of your animal are necessary for pleasure. What is said about overloading applies here: you must go light; let your saddlebags be small, and packed so as not to chafe the horse. If you have the choice of a saddle, take a "McClellan" or a similar one, so that you can easily strap on your blankets and bags. If you have time before starting, try to teach your horse, what so few horses in the Northern States know, to be guided by the pressure of reins against the neck instead of a pull at the bit.

### BOATING.

I do not propose to say much about boating, as the subject can hardly have justice done to it in a book of this sort. Parties of young men spend their summer vacation every year in camping and boating. It is a most delightful way,— superior in many respects to any other, — but it requires both experience and caution, neither of which is usually found in young men. So I hope that, if you will go in a boat, you may be an exception to the general rule, and will, for your parents' and friends' sake, take a small boat without ballast rather than a large one ballasted so heavily that it will sink when it fills.

When you belay the sheets of your sail, make a knot that can be untied by a single pull at the loose end: any boatman will show you how to do this. *Never make fast the sheets in any other way.* Hold the sheets in your hands if the wind is at all squally or strong. Do not venture out in a heavy wind. Stow your baggage snugly before you start: tubs made by sawing a flour-barrel in two are excellent to throw loose stuff into. Remember to be careful; keep your eyes open, and know what you are going to do before you try it. The saying of an old sea-captain comes to me here: "I would rather sail a ship around the world, than to go down the bay in a boat sailed by a boy."

### RECKONING LOST.

It often happens in travelling, that the sun rises in what appears the north, west, or south, and we seem to be moving in the wrong direction, so that when we return home our remembrance of the journey is confused. Perhaps a few hints on this subject may help the reader. Supposing your day's journey ends at Blanktown, where you find your compass-points apparently reversed. It then becomes natural for you to make matters worse by trying to lay out in your mind a new map, with Blanktown for the "hub," and east in the west, and so on. You can often prevent these mishaps, and can always make them less annoying, by studying your map well both before and during your journey; and by keeping in your mind continually, with all the vividness you can, what you are really doing. As far as Blanktown is concerned, you will have two impressions, just as we all have two impressions with regard to the revolution of the earth on its axis: apparently the sun rises, goes over and down; but in our minds we can see the sun standing still, and the earth turning from west to east.

Upon leaving Blanktown you are likely to carry the error along with you, and to find yourself moving in what appears to be the wrong way. Keep in mind with all the vividness possible, the picture of what you are really doing, and keep out of mind as much as you can the ugly appearance of going the wrong way. Every important change you make, be sure to "see it" in the mind's eye, and let the natural eye be blind to all that is deceiving. After a while things will grow real, and you must try to keep them so. The more perfectly you know the route and all its details, the less you will be troubled in this way.

If you are travelling in the cars, and if you have a strong power of imagination, you can very easily right errors of this kind by learning from the map exactly what you are doing, and then by sitting next to the window, shut your eyes as you go around a curve that tends to aggravate the difficulty, and hold fast what you get on curves that help you. If you sit on the left side of the car, and look ahead, the cars seem to sweep continually a little to the right, and *vice versa*, when really moving straight ahead,—provided your imagination is good.

When you are travelling on an unknown road, you should always inquire all about it, to avoid taking the wrong one, which you are likely to do, even if you have a good map with you.

### LADIES AS PEDESTRIANS.

I have once or twice alluded to ladies walking and camping. It is thoroughly practicable for them to do so. They must have a wagon, and do none of the heavy work; their gowns must not reach quite to the ground, and all of their clothing must be loose and easy.[1] Of course there must be gentlemen in the party; and it may save annoyance to have at least one of the ladies well-nigh "middle-aged." Ladies must be cared for more tenderly than men. If they are not well, the wagon should go back for them at the end of the day's march; shelter-tents are not to be recommended for them, nor are two blankets sufficient bedclothing. They ought not to be compelled to go any definite distance, but after having made their day's walk let the tents be pitched. Rainy weather is particularly unpleasant to ladies in tents; deserted houses, schoolhouses, saw-mills, or barns should be sought for them when a storm is brewing.

### LADIES AND CHILDREN IN CAMP.

In a permanent camp, however, ladies, and children as well, can make themselves thoroughly at home.[2] They ought not to "rough it" so

---

[1] A flannel dress, the skirt coming to the top of the boots, and having a blouse waist, will be found most comfortable.

[2] It is no novelty for women and children to camp out: we see them every summer at the seaside and on the blueberry-plains. A great many families besides live in rude cabins, which are preferable on many accounts, but are expensive. Sickness sometimes results, but usually all are much benefited. I know a family that numbered with its guests nine ladies, five children ("one at the breast"), and the *paterfamilias*, which camped several weeks through some of the best and some of the worst of weather. The whooping-cough broke out

much as young men expect to: consequently they should be better protected from the wet and cold.

I have seen a man with his wife and two children enjoy themselves through a week of rainy weather in an A-tent; but there are not many such happy families, and it is not advisable to camp with such limited accommodations.

Almost all women will find it trying to their backs to be kept all day in an A-tent. If you have no other kind, you should build some sort of a wall, and pitch the tent on top of it. It is not a difficult or expensive task to put guy-lines and a wall of drilling on an A-tent, and make new poles, or pitch the old ones upon posts. In either case you should stay the tent with lines running from the top to the ground.

It has already been advised that women should have a stove; in general, they ought not to depart so far from home ways as men do.

Rubber boots are almost a necessity for women and children during rainy weather and while the dew is upon the grass.

the second or third day; shortly after, the tent of the mother and children blew down in the night, and turned them all out into the pelting rain in their night-clothes. Excepting the misery of that night and day, nothing serious came of it; and in the fall all returned home better every way for having spent their summer in camp.

### SUMMER-HOUSES, SHEDS, AND BRUSH SCREENS.

There is little to be said of the summer-houses built at the seaside near our large cities, since that is rather a matter of carpentry; nor of portable houses; nor of lattice-work with painted paper; nor even of a "schbang" such as I have often built of old doors, shutters, outer windows, and tarred paper: any one who is ingenious can knock together all the shelter his needs require or means allow. But, where you are camping for a week or more, it pays you well to use all you have in making yourself comfortable. A bush house, a canopy under which to eat, and something better than plain "out-of-doors" to cook in, are among the first things to attend to.

If you wish to plant firmly a tree that you have cut down, you may perhaps be able to drive a stake larger than the trunk of the tree; then loosen the stake by hitting it on the sides, and pull it out. You can do this when you have no shovel, or when the soil is too hard to dig. Small stakes wedged down the hole after putting in the tree will make it firm.

### ETIQUETTE.

Some things considered essential at the home table have fallen into disuse in camp. It is pardonable, and perhaps best, to bring on whatever you have cooked in the dish that it is cooked in, so as to prevent its cooling off.

You will also be allowed to help yourself first to whatever is nearest you, before passing it to another; for passing things around in camp is risky, and should be avoided as much as possible for that reason.

Eat with your hats on, as it is more comfortable, and the wind is not so apt to blow your stray hairs into the next man's dish.

If you have no fork, do not mind eating with your knife and fingers. But, however much liberty you take, do not be rude, coarse, or uncivil: these bad habits grow rapidly in camp if you encourage them, and are broken off with difficulty on return.

If there is no separate knife for the butter, cheese, and meat, nor spoon for the gravy and soup, you can use your own by first wiping the knife or spoon upon a piece of bread.

Be social and agreeable to all fellow-travellers you meet. It is a received rule now, I believe, that you are under no obligations to consider travelling-acquaintances as permanent: so you are in duty bound to be friendly to all thrown in your way. However, it is not fair to thrust your company upon others, nor compel a courtesy from any one. Try to remember too, that it is nothing wonderful to camp out or walk; and do not expect any one to think it is. We frequently meet parties of young folks walking through the mountains, who do great things with their tongues, but not much with their feet. If you will refrain from bragging, you can speak of your short marches without exciting contempt.

Avoid as much as possible asking another member of the party to do your work, or to wait upon you: it is surprising how easily you can make yourself disliked by asking a few trifling favors of one who is tired and hungry.

### MOSQUITOES, BLACK FLIES, AND MIDGE.

These pests will annoy you exceedingly almost everywhere in the summer. In the daytime motion and perspiration keep them off to some extent. At night, or when lying down, you can do no better than to cover yourself so that they cannot reach your body, and have a mosquito-bar of some sort over your head. The simplest thing is a square yard of mosquito-netting thrown over the head, and tucked in well. You will need to have your hat first thrown over the head, and your shirt-collar turned up, to prevent the mosquitoes reaching through the mesh to your face and neck.

A better way than this is to make a box-shaped mosquito-bar, large enough to stretch across the head of the bed, and cover the heads and shoulders of all that sleep in the tent. It should be six or eight feet long, twenty to twenty-six inches wide, and one yard or more high. It will be more durable, but not quite so well ventilated, if the top is made of light cloth instead of netting. The seams should be bound with stout tape, and the sides and ends "gathered" considerably in sewing them to the top. Even then the side that falls over the shoulders of the sleepers may not be loose enough to fill the hollows between them; the netting will then have to be tucked under the blanket, or have something thrown over its lower edge.

Sew loops or strings on the four upper corners, and corresponding loops or strings on the tent, so that you can tie up the bar.

Bobbinet lace is better than the common netting for all of these purposes. It comes in pieces twelve to fourteen yards long, and two yards wide. You cannot often find it for sale; but the large shops in the principal cities that do a great business by correspondence can send it to you.

Oil of cedar and oil of pennyroyal are recommended as serviceable in driving off mosquitoes, and there are patented compounds whose labels pretend great things: you will try them only once, I think.

Ammoniated opodeldoc rubbed upon the bites

will in a great measure stop the itching, and hasten the cure.

They say that a little gunpowder flashed in the tent will drive out flies and mosquitoes. I saw a man try it once, but noticed that he himself went out in a great hurry, while the flies, if they went at all, were back again before he was.

A better thing, really the best, is a smudge made by building a small fire to the windward of your tent, and nearly smothering it with chips, moss, bark, or rotten wood. If you make the smudge in an old pan or pot, you can move it about as often as the wind changes.

### HOW TO SKIN FISH.

When you camp by the seaside, you will catch cunners and other fish that need skinning. Let no one persuade you to slash the back fins out with a single stroke, as you would whittle a stick; but take a sharp knife, cut on both sides of the fin, and then pull out the whole of it from head to tail, and thus save the trouble that a hundred little bones will make if left in. After cutting the skin on the under side from head to tail, and taking out the entrails and small fins, start the skin where the head joins the body, and pull it off one side at a time. Some men stick an awl through a cunner's head, or catch it fast in a stout iron hook, to hold it while skinning.

Cunners and lobsters are sometimes caught off bold rocks in a net. You can make one easily out of a hogshead-hoop, and twine stretched across so as to make a three-inch mesh.[1] Tie a lot of bait securely in the middle, sink it for a few minutes, and draw up rapidly. The rush of water through the net prevents the fish from escaping.

### EXPENSES.

The expenses of camping or walking vary greatly, of course, according to the route, manner of going, and other things. The principal items are railroad-tickets, horse and wagon hire, trucking, land-rent (if you camp where rent is charged), and the cost of the outfit. You ought to be able to reckon very nearly what you will have to pay on account of these before you spend a cent. After this will come the calculation whether to travel at all by rail, supposing you wish to go a hundred miles to reach the seaside where you propose to camp, or the mountains you want to climb. If you have a horse and wagon, or are going horseback, it will doubtless be cheaper to march than to ride and pay freight. If time is plenty and money is

---

[1] The mesh of a net is measured by pulling it diagonally as far as possible, and finding the distance from knot to knot; consequently a three-inch mesh will open so as to make a square of about an inch and a half.

scarce, you may perhaps be able to walk the distance cheaper than to go by rail; but, if you lodge at hotels, you will find it considerably more expensive. The question then is apt to turn on whether the hundred miles is worth seeing, and whether it is so thickly settled as to prevent your camping.

To walk a hundred miles, carrying your kit all the way, will take from one to two weeks, according to your age, strength, and the weather. We have already stated that there is little *pleasure* in walking more than sixty miles a week. But if you wish to go as fast as you can, and have taken pains to practise walking before starting, and can buy your food in small quantities daily, and can otherwise reduce your baggage, you can make the hundred miles in a week without difficulty, and more if it is necessary, unless there is much bad weather.

The expense for food will also vary according to one's will; but it need not be heavy if you can content yourself with simple fare. You can hardly live at a cheaper rate than the following:—

ONE WEEK'S SUPPLY FOR TWO MEN.

Ten pounds of pilot-bread; eight pounds of salt pork; one pound of coffee (roasted and ground); one to two pounds of sugar (granulated); thirty pounds of potatoes (half a bushel).[1] A little beef and butter, and a few ginger-snaps, will be good investments.

Supposing you and I were to start from home in the morning after breakfast; when noon comes, we eat the lunch we have taken with us, and press on. As the end of the day's march approaches, we look out to buy two quarts of potatoes at a farmhouse or store; and we boil or fry, or boil and mash in milk, enough of these for our supper. The breakfast next morning is much the same. We cook potatoes in every way we know, and eat the whole of our stock remaining, thus saving so much weight to carry. We also soak some pilot-bread, and fry that for a dessert, eating a little sugar on it if we can spare it. When dinner-time approaches, we keep a lookout for a chance to buy ten or twelve cents' worth of bread or biscuits. These are more palatable than the pilot-bread or crackers in our haversack. If we have a potato left from breakfast, we cook and eat it now. We cut off a slice of the corned beef, and take a nibble at the ginger-snaps. If we think we can afford three or four cents more, we buy a pint of milk,

---

[1] The field allowance in the United States army is nearly 1¼ pounds of coffee and 2¼ pounds of sugar (damp brown) for two men seven days; the bread and pork ration is also larger than that above given; but the allowance of potatoes is almost nothing.

and make a little dip-toast. And so we go; sometimes we catch a fish, or pass an orchard whose owner gives us all the windfalls we want. We pick berries too; and keep a sharp lookout that we supply ourselves in season when our pilot-bread, sugar, pork, and butter run low. Some days we overtake farmers driving ox-carts or wagons; we throw our kits aboard, and walk slowly along, willing to lose a little time to save our aching shoulders. And in due time, if no accident befalls, nor rainy weather detains us, we arrive at our seashore or mountain.

You may like to know that this is almost an exact history, at least as far as eating is concerned, of a twelve days' tramp I once went on in company with two other boys. There was about five dollars in the party, and nearly two dollars of this was spent in paying toll on a boat that we took through a canal a part of the way. We carried coffee, sugar, pork, and beef from home, and ate potatoes three times a day. We had a delightful time, and came home fattened up somewhat; but I will admit that I did not call for potatoes when I got back to my father's table, for some days.

In general, however, it will be noticed that those who camp out for the season, or go on walking-tours, do so at a moderate expense because they start with the determination to make it cheap. For this purpose they content themselves with old clothes, which they fit over or repair, take cooking-utensils from their own kitchen, and, excepting in the matter of canned foods, do not live very differently from what they do at home.

Nearly all the parties of boys that I have questioned spend all the money they have, be it little or much. Generally those I have met walking or camping seem to be impressed with the magnitude of their operations, and to be carrying constantly with them the determination to spend their funds sparingly enough to reach home without begging. It is not bad practice for a young man.

Here I wish to say a word to parents — having been a boy myself, and being now a father. Let your boys go when summer comes; put them to their wits; do not let them be extravagant, nor have money to pay other men for working for them. It is far better for them to move about than to remain in one place all the time. The last, especially if the camp is near some place of public resort, tends to encourage idleness and dissipation.

When you return home again from a tour of camping, and go back to a sedentary life, remember that you do not need to eat all that your appetite calls for. You may make yourself sick if you go on eating such meals as you have been digesting in camp. You are apt also upon your return to feel as you did on the first and second days of your tour; this is especially liable to be the case if you have overworked yourself, or have not had enough sleep.

## CHAPTER XI.

#### DIARY.

By all means keep a diary: the act of writing will help you to remember these good times, and the diary will prove the pleasantest of reading in after-years. It is not an easy thing to write in camp or on the march, but if it costs you an effort you will prize it all the more. I beg you to persevere, and, if you fail, to " try, try again." I cannot overcome the desire to tell you the results of my experience in diary-writing; for I have tried it long, and under many different circumstances. They are as follows:—

First, any thing written at the time is far better than no record at all; so, if you can only write a pocket diary with lead pencil, do that.

Second, All such small diaries, scraps, letters, and every thing written illegibly or with lead pencil, are difficult to preserve or to read, and are very unhandy for reference.

Third, It is great folly to persuade yourself that after taking notes for a week or two, or writing a hurried sketch, you can extend or copy and illuminate at your leisure.

Consequently, write what you can, and let it stand with all its blots, errors, and nonsense. And be careful, when you are five years older, not to go through the diary with eraser and scissors; for, if you live still another five years, nothing will interest you more than this diary with all its defects.

I find after having written many diaries of many forms, that I have now to regret I did not at first choose some particular size, say "letter-size," and so have had all my diaries uniform. I will never again use "onion-skin," which is too thin, nor any odd-shaped, figured, cheap, or colored paper. I do not like those large printed diaries which give you just a page or half-page a day, nor a paper whose ruling shows conspicuously.

I like best when at home to write in a blank book; and when I go off on a summer vacation I leave that diary safely at home, and take a portfolio with some sheets of blank paper upon which to write the diary, and mail them as fast as written. These answer for letters to the friends at home, and save writing any more to them. They also, when bound, form a diary exclusively of travels. When I return I write an epitome in the home-diary, and thus prevent a break of dates in that book. The paper for the diary of travels is strong, but rather thin and white. I buy enough of it at once to make a volume, and thus have the diary sheets uniform.

I am quite sure that you will do well to write a diary of your summer vacation, upon the plan just named, whether you keep one at home or not. Try to do it well, but do not undertake too much. Write facts such as what you saw, heard, did, and failed to do; but do not try to write poetry or fine writing of any kind. Mention what kind of weather; but do not attempt a meteorological record unless you have a special liking for that science. If you camp in Jacob Sawyer's pasture, and he gives you a quart of milk, say so, instead of "a good old man showed us a favor;" for in after-years the memory of it will be sweeter than the milk was, and it will puzzle you to recall the "good old man's" name and what the favor was. If you have time, try to draw: never mind if it is a poor picture. I have some of the strangest-looking portraits and most surprising perspectives in my diaries written when fifteen to twenty years old; but I would not exchange them now for one of the "old masters." Do not neglect the narrative, however, for sake of drawing.

I have noticed that when my paper is down in the bottom of a valise, and the pen in a wallet, and the penholder in a coat-pocket, and portfolio somewhere else, it is not so easy to "find time to write" as when I have penholder, pen, and paper in the portfolio, and the portfolio and ink in my haversack. Under these favorable conditions it is easy to snatch a few moments from any halt; and a diary written on the spur of the moment is a diary that will be worth reading in after-life. If it is impossible, however, as it so often is, to write oftener than once a day, you will do well to make a note of events as fast as they happen, so that you shall not forget them, nor have to stop to recall them when your time is precious.

I have heard of diaries with side-notes on each page, and even an index at the end of the book; but not many men, and but few boys, can do all this; and my advice to the average boy is, not to undertake it, nor any thing else that will use the time, patience, and perseverance, needed to write the narrative.

You will find it convenient for reference if you make a paragraph of every subject. Date every day distinctly, with a much bolder handwriting than the body of the diary; and write the date on the right margin of the right page, and left margin of the left page, with the year at the top of the page only. Skip a line or two instead of ruling between the days. Thus:—

                                    **1878.**
*Pleasant and mild.*                **JANUARY 1,**
*Vacation ends to-day.*             **SATURDAY.**

*Jo. Harding is full of going on a walk to the White Mountains next summer, and he wants me to go too.*

*Made New-Year calls on Susie Smith, Mary Lyman, Ellen Jenkins, Christie Jameson, and Martha Buzzell.*

*Warm again and misty.*             **JANUARY 2,**
*Went to church. Mr. Simpson's pup followed* **SUNDAY.**
*him in; and it took Simpson, Jenks the sexton, and two small boys, to put him out.*

*Accompanied Susie Smith to the Baptist's this evening, and went home by way of Centre Street to avoid the crowd. Crowds are not so bad sometimes.*

*Still mild and pleasant, but cooler.*  **JANUARY 3,**
*Went to school, and failed in algebra. This* **MONDAY.**
X *business is too much for me.*

*Abel's shoe-factory, next to our schoolhouse, caught fire this afternoon while we were at recess, and Mr. Nason dismissed the school. We all hurrahed for Nason, and went to the fire. Steamer No. 1 put it out in less than ten minutes after she got there.*

*Home all the evening, studying.*

If you are like me, you will be glad by and by if you note in your diary of the summer vacation a few dry statistics, such as distances walked, names of people you meet, steamers you take passage on, and, in general, every thing that interested you at the time, even to the songs you sing; for usually some few songs run in your head all through the tour, and it is pleasant to recall them in after-years.

Do not write so near the margins of the paper that the binder will cut off the writing when he comes to trim them.

# CHAPTER XII.

## "HOW TO DO IT."

THE following advice by Rev. Edward Everett Hale is so good that I have appropriated it. You will find more good advice in the same book.[1]

"First, never walk before breakfast. If you like you may make two breakfasts, and take a mile or two between; but be sure to eat something before you are on the road.

"Second, do not walk much in the middle of the day. It is dusty and hot then; and the landscape has lost its special glory. By ten o'clock you ought to have found some camping-ground for the day,—a nice brook running through a grove; a place to draw, or paint, or tell stories, or read them or write them; a place to make waterfalls and dams, to sail chips, or build boats; a place to make a fire and a cup of tea for the oldsters. Stay here till four in the afternoon, and then push on in the two or three

[1] How to Do It. Published by Roberts Brothers, Boston.

hours which are left to the sleeping-place agreed upon. Four or five hours on the road is all you want in each day. Even resolute idlers, as it is to be hoped you all are on such occasions, can get eight miles a day out of that; and that is enough for a true walking-party. Remember all along that you are not running a race with the railway-train. If you were, you would be beaten certainly; and the less you think you are, the better. You are travelling in a method of which the merit is that it is not fast, and that you see every separate detail of the glory of the world. What a fool you are, then, if you tire yourself to death, merely that you may say that you did in ten hours what the locomotive would gladly have finished in one, if by that effort you have lost exactly the enjoyment of nature and society that you started for!"

The advice to rest in the heat of the day is good for very hot weather; young people, however, are too impatient to follow it unless there is an apparent necessity. The feeling at twelve o'clock that you have yet to walk as far as you have come is not so pleasant as that of knowing you have all the afternoon for rest. For this reason nearly every one will finish the walk as soon as possible; still Mr. Hale's plan is a good one — the best for very hot weather.

## STILL ANOTHER WAY TO TRAVEL.

Mr. Hale also tells an amusing story of his desire when young to sail down the Connecticut River; but he was dissuaded from doing so when the chance finally came, by people who thought the road was the only place to travel in. And now he is sorry he did not sail.

The reading of his story brings to mind a similar experience that I had when young, and it is now one of the keen regrets of my manhood, that I likewise was laughed out of a boyish plan that would have given me untold pleasure and profit had it been carried out. I loved to walk, and I wanted to see the towns within a circuit of twenty or thirty miles of home ; but I could not afford to pay hotel-bills, and I was not strong enough to carry a camping-outfit. But I had an old cart, strong and large enough to hold all I should need. I could load it with the same food that I should eat if I staid at home; could wear my old clothes, take my oilcloth overcoat, an axe, frying-pan, pail, and a borrowed tent and poles ; and I would learn the county by heart before vacation was over, and not cost my father a cent more than if I staid at home. Oh, why didn't I go! Simply because I was laughed out of it. I was told that people did not travel in that way ; I should be arrested; the boys would hoot at and stone me; the men would set their dogs on me; I should be driven out of my camping-place; thieves would steal my seventy-five cent cart; dogs would eat up my stock of food; and the first man who overtook me would tell the people that a crazy boy from Portland was coming along the road dragging a baby-wagon, whereupon every woman would leave her kitchen, and every man his field, to see and laugh at me. But, above all, the thing would be known in our neighborhood, and the boys and girls would join in their abuse of the county explorer.

That was the end of it; the being made sport of by *my own friends*, and hearing the *small boys in our street* sing out "How's your cart?" and to be known all through life perhaps as "*one-horse John*" — the punishment would be too severe.

But, my young friends, I made a great mistake; and I want to caution you *not* to surrender to any such nonsense as I did. If you wish to go to sea in a skiff, it is well to give in to a fisherman's advice to stay at home, for he can assure you that winds and waves will be the death of you; but if you have a good hand-wagon, and are willing to stand a few taunts, by all means go on your walk, and pull your wagon after you. You will learn a lesson in independence that will be of value to you, if you learn nothing else.

# CHAPTER XIII.

### HYGIENIC NOTES.

[This chapter is taken in full from a work on ornithology, written by Dr. Coues of the Smithsonian Institution. It is the advice of an accomplished naturalist and sportsman to his fellow-naturalists, but is equally adapted to the young camper. Hardly any one can write more understandingly on the subjects here presented than the doctor, who has had long experience with the army, both in the field and garrison, and is an enthusiastic student of natural history besides. The remarks upon alcoholic stimulants are especially recommended to the reader, coming as they do from an army officer, and not a temperance reformer.

Those who wish to become familiar with the details of bird-collecting will find a treasure in the doctor's book, "Field Ornithology, comprising a Manual of Instruction for procuring, preparing, and preserving Birds; and a check list of North American Birds. By Dr. Elliott Coues, U.S.A. Salem: Naturalists' Agency."]

### ACCIDENTS.

THE secret of safe *climbing* is never to relax one hold until another is secured; it is in spirit equally applicable to scrambling over rocks, a particularly difficult thing to do safely with a loaded gun. Test rotten, slippery, or otherwise suspicious holds, before trusting them. In lifting the body up anywhere, keep the mouth shut, breathe through the nostrils, and go slowly.

In *swimming* waste no strength unnecessarily in trying to stem a current; yield partly, and land obliquely lower down; if exhausted, float: the slightest motion of the hands will ordinarily keep the face above water; in any event keep your wits collected. In fording deeply, a heavy stone [in the hands, above water] will strengthen your position.

Never sail a boat experimentally: if you are no sailor, take one with you, or stay on land.

In crossing a high narrow foot-path, never look lower than your feet; the muscles will work true if not confused with faltering instructions from a giddy brain. On soft ground see what, if any thing, has preceded you; large hoof-marks generally mean that the way is safe: if none are found, inquire for yourself before going on. Quicksand is the most treacherous because far more dangerous than it looks; but I have seen a mule's ears finally disappear in genuine mud.

Cattle-paths, however erratic, commonly prove the surest way out of a difficult place, whether of uncertain footing or dense undergrowth.

### "TAKING COLD."

This vague "household word" indicates one or more of a long varied train of unpleasant affections nearly always traceable to one or the other of only two causes, — *sudden change* of temperature, and *unequal distribution* of temperature. No extremes of heat or cold can alone affect this result: persons frozen to death do not "take cold" during the process. But if a part of the body be rapidly cooled, as by evaporation from a wet article of clothing, or by sitting in a draught of air, the rest of the body remaining at an ordinary temperature; or if the temperature. of the whole be suddenly changed by going out into the cold, or especially by coming into a warm room, — there is much liability of trouble.

There is an old saying, —

> "When the air comes through a hole,
> Say your prayers to save your soul."

And I should think almost any one could get a "cold" with a spoonful of water on the wrist held to a key-hole. Singular as it may seem, sudden warming when cold is more dangerous than the reverse: every one has noticed how soon the handkerchief is required on entering a heated room on a cold day. Frost-bite is an extreme illustration of this. As the Irishman said on picking himself up, it was not the fall, but stopping so quickly, that hurt him: it is not the lowering of the temperature to freezing point, but its subsequent elevation, that devitalizes the tissue. This is why rubbing with snow, or bathing in cold water, is required to restore safely a frozen part: the arrested circulation must be very gradually re-established, or inflammation, perhaps mortification, ensues.

General precautions against taking cold are almost self-evident in this light. There is ordinarily little if any danger to be apprehended from wet clothes, so long as exercise is kept up; for the "glow" about compensates for the extra cooling by evaporation. Nor is a complete drenching more likely to be injurious than wetting of one part. But never sit still wet, and in changing rub the body dry. There is a general tendency, springing from fatigue, indolence, or indifference, to neglect damp feet, — that is to say, to dry them by the fire; but this process is tedious and uncertain. I would say especially, "Off with muddy boots and sodden socks at once:" dry stockings and slippers after a hunt may make just the difference of your being able to go out again, or never. Take care never to check perspiration: during this process the body is in a somewhat critical condition, and the sudden arrest of the function may result disastrously, even fatally. One part of the business of perspiration is to equalize bodily temperature, and it must not be interfered with. The secret of much that is said about *bathing* when heated lies here. A person overheated, panting it may be, with throbbing temples and a *dry* skin, is in danger partly because the natural cooling by evaporation from the skin is denied; and this condition is sometimes not far from a "sunstroke." Under these circumstances, a person of fairly good constitution may plunge into the water with impunity, even with benefit. But, if the body be already cooling by sweating, rapid abstraction of heat from the surface may cause internal congestion, never unattended with danger.

Drinking ice-water offers a somewhat parallel case; even on stopping to drink at the brook, when flushed with heat, it is well to bathe the face and hands first, and to taste the water before a full draught. It is a well-known excellent rule, not to bathe immediately after a full meal; because during digestion the organs concerned are comparativey engorged and any sudden disturbance of the circulation may be disastrous.

The imperative necessity of resisting drowsiness under extreme cold requires no comment.

In walking under a hot sun, the head may be sensibly protected by green leaves or grass in the hat; they may be advantageously moistened, but not enough to drip about the ears. Under such circumstances the slightest giddiness, dimness of sight, or confusion of ideas, should be taken as a warning of possible sunstroke, instantly demanding rest, and shelter if practicable.

### HUNGER AND FATIGUE

are more closely related than they might seem to be: one is a sign that the fuel is out, and the other asks for it. Extreme fatigue, indeed, destroys appetite: this simply means temporary incapacity for digestion. But, even far short of this, food is more easily digested and better relished after a little preparation of the furnace. On coming home tired it is much better to make a leisurely and reasonably nice toilet, than to eat at once, or to lie still thinking how tired you are; after a change and a wash you feel like a "new man," and go to the table in capital state. Whatever dietetic irregularities a high state of civilization may demand or render practicable, a normally healthy person is inconvenienced almost as soon as his regular mealtime passes without food; and few can work comfortably or profitably fasting over six or eight hours. Eat before starting; if for a day's tramp, take a lunch; the most frugal meal will appease if it do not satisfy hunger, and so postpone its urgency. As a small scrap of practical wisdom, I would add, Keep the remnants of the lunch if there be any; for you cannot always be sure of getting in to supper.

## STIMULATION.

When cold, fatigued, depressed in mind, and on other occasions, you may feel inclined to resort to artificial stimulus. Respecting this many-sided theme I have a few words to offer — of direct bearing on the collector's case. It should be clearly understood, in the first place, that a stimulant confers no strength whatever: it simply calls the powers that be into increased action, at their own expense. Seeking real strength in stimulus is as wise as an attempt to lift yourself up by your boot-straps. You may gather yourself to leap the ditch, and you clear it; but no such muscular energy can be sustained: exhaustion speedily renders further expenditure impossible. But now suppose a very powerful mental impression be made, say the circumstance of a succession of ditches in front, and a mad dog behind: if the stimulus of terror be sufficiently strong, you may leap on till you drop senseless. Alcoholic stimulus is a parallel case, and is not seldom pushed to the same extreme. Under its influence you never can tell when you *are* tired; the expenditure goes on, indeed, with unnatural rapidity, only it is not felt at the time; but the upshot is, you have all the original fatigue to endure and to recover from, *plus* the fatigue resulting from over-excitation of the system. Taken as a fortification against cold, alcohol is as unsatisfactory as a remedy for fatigue. Insensibility to cold does not imply protection. The fact is, the exposure is greater than before; the circulation and respiration being hurried, the waste is greater; and, as sound fuel cannot be immediately supplied, the temperature of the body is soon lowered. The transient warmth and glow over the system has both cold *and* depression to endure. There is no use in borrowing from yourself, and fancying you are richer.

Secondly, the value of any stimulus (except in a few exigencies of disease or injury) is in proportion, not to the intensity, but to the equableness and durability, of its effect. This is one reason why tea, coffee, and articles of corresponding qualities, are preferable to alcoholic drinks: they work so smoothly that their effect is often unnoticed, and they "stay by" well. The friction of alcohol is tremendous in comparison. A glass of grog may help a veteran over the fence; but no one, young or old, can shoot all day on whiskey.

I have had so much experience in the use of tobacco as a mild stimulant, that I am probably no impartial judge of its merits. I will simply say, I do not use it in the field, because it indisposes to muscular activity, and favors reflection when observation is required; and because temporary abstinence provokes the morbid appetite, and renders the weed more grateful afterwards.

Thirdly, undue excitation of any physical function is followed by a corresponding depression, on the simple principle that action and reaction are equal; and the balance of health turns too easily to be wilfully disturbed. Stimulation is a draft upon vital capital, when interest alone should suffice: it may be needed at times to bridge a chasm; but habitual living beyond vital income infallibly entails bankruptcy in health. The use of alcohol in health seems practically restricted to purposes of sensuous gratification on the part of those prepared to pay a round price for this luxury. The three golden rules here are, — Never drink before breakfast; never drink alone; and never drink bad liquor. Their observance may make even the abuse of alcohol tolerable. Serious objections, for a naturalist at least, are that science, viewed through a glass, seems distant and uncertain, while the joys of rum are immediate and unquestionable; and that intemperance, being an attempt to defy certain physical laws, is therefore eminently unscientific.

Besides the above good advice by Dr. Coues, the following may prove useful to the camper: —

Diarrhœa may result from overwork and gluttony combined, and from eating indigestible or uncooked food, and from imperfect protection of the stomach. "Remove the cause, and the effect will cease." A flannel bandage six to twelve inches wide, worn around the stomach, is good as a preventive and cure.

The same causes may produce cholera morbus; symptoms, violent vomiting and purging, faintness, and spasms in the arms and limbs. Unless accompanied with cramp (which is not usual), nature will work its own cure. Give warm drinks if you have them. Do not get frightened, but keep the patient warm, and well protected from a draught of air.

The liability to costiveness, and the remedies therefor, are noted on p. 55 of this book.

A very rare occurrence, but a constant dread with some people, is an insect crawling into the ear. If you have oil, spirits of turpentine, or alcoholic liquor at hand, fill the ear at once. If you have not these, use coffee, tea, warm water (not too hot), or almost any liquid which is not hurtful to the skin.

## MARSHALL HALL'S READY METHOD IN SUFFOCATION, DROWNING, ETC.

1st, Treat the patient *instantly on the spot*, in the *open air*, freely exposing the face, neck, and chest to the breeze, except in severe weather.

2d, In order *to clear the throat*, place the patient gently on the face, with one wrist under the forehead, that all fluid, and the tongue itself, may fall forward, and leave the entrance into the windpipe free.

3d, *To excite respiration*, turn the patient slightly on his side, and apply some irritating or stimulating agent to the nostrils, as *veratrine, dilute ammonia*, &c.

4th, Make the face warm by brisk friction; then dash cold water upon it.

5th, If not successful, lose no time; but, *to imitate respiration*, place the patient on his face, and turn the body gently but completely *on the side and a little beyond*, then again on the face, and so on alternately. Repeat these movements deliberately and perseveringly, *fifteen times only* in a minute. (When the patient lies on the thorax, this cavity is *compressed* by the weight of the body, and *ex*piration takes place. When he is turned on the side, this pressure is removed, and *in*spiration occurs.)

6th, When the prone position is resumed, make a uniform and efficient pressure *along the spine*, removing the pressure immediately, before rotation on the side. (The pressure augments the *ex*piration, the rotation commences *in*spiration.) Continue these measures.

7th, Rub the limbs *upward*, with *firm pressure*

and with *energy*. (The object being to aid the return of venous blood to the heart.)

8th, Substitute for the patient's wet clothing, if possible, such other covering as can be instantly procured, each bystander supplying a coat or cloak, &c. Meantime, and from time to time, *to excite inspiration*, let the surface of the body be *slapped* briskly with the hand.

9th, Rub the body briskly till it is dry and warm, then dash *cold* water upon it, and repeat the rubbing.

Avoid the immediate removal of the patient, as it involves a *dangerous loss of time;* also the use of bellows or any *forcing* instrument ; also the *warm bath* and *all rough treatment.*

### POISONS.

In all cases of poisoning, the first step is to evacuate the stomach. This should be effected by an emetic which is *quickly* obtained, and most powerful and speedy in its operation. Such are, powdered mustard (a large tablespoonful in a tumblerful of warm water), powdered alum (in half-ounce doses), sulphate of zinc (ten to thirty grains), tartar emetic (one to two grains) combined with powdered ipecacuanha (twenty grains), and sulphate of copper (two to five grains). When vomiting has already taken place, copious draughts of warm water or warm mucilaginous drinks should be given, to keep up the effect till the poisoning substance has been thoroughly evacuated.

## PARTING ADVICE.

Be independent, but not impudent. See all you can, and make the most of your time; "time is money;" and, when you grow older, you may find it even more difficult to command time than money.

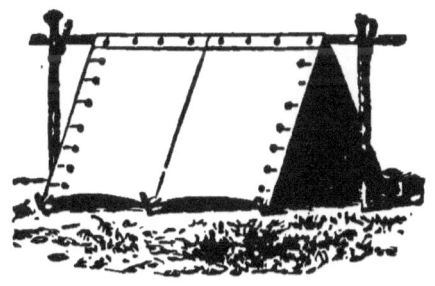

# INDEX.

Accidents, boy run over, 34.
    how to avoid, 117.
Advice to parents, 105.
Afoot, ways to travel, 9-24.
Alcoholic stimulants, 55, 123.
Ammoniated opoldeldoc for bites, 99.
Appetite, none first days, 55.
    on return home, 105.
A-tents, 75-79, 95.
    too small for ladies, 95.
Babies in camp, 94.
Baggage: —
  Barrel, 32.
  Blanket, 16-19.
  Candles and lamps, 61.
  Clothing, 35-38.
  Cooking utensils, 42-46.
  Cover for wagon, 25.
  Food, 20, 47-49.
  Haversack, 18.
  Knapsack, 16.
  Ladies' outfits, 94.
  Mattress, 63.
  Overcoat, 19, 58.
  Overloading, 15, 90.
  Packing a wagon, 26, 32.
  Poles, 60, 73.
  Pork, how carried, 48.
  Shirts, 19.
  Stove, 39-41.
  Tents, 72-80.
  Tub, 91.
  Wagon, 31-33.
Baked beans, beef, and fish, 46.
Baker, Yankee, 43.
Barrel, on march for baggage, 32.
    sunk for cellar, 48.
    cut in two for tubs, 91.
Bathing, 52, 53, 64, 120.
Beans and pork, how baked, 46.
Beckets for tents, 79, 81.

Beds, 62-64.
Black flies, protection from, 98.
Blanket, woollen, 19, 22, 25, 94.
  instead of knapsack, 16.
  lining, 19.
  rubber, 16, 22, 75.
Board floor for tent, 60.
Boat, don't sail experimentally, 118.
Boating, general advice, 90.
Bobbinet lace mosquito-bar, 99.
Boots and brogans, 36, 37.
Brush or bush houses, 69, 96.
Bug in ear, 126.
Bumpers for wagon-springs, 31.
Butter, how to keep, 47.
Camp, 60-71.
  Beds, 62-64.
  Brush-houses, 69, 96.
  Candles and sluts, 62.
  Care of food, 47-49.
  Cellar, 48.
  Children, 94.
  Clothes-line, 61, 64.
  Cold weather, 66.
  Cooking, 44, 47.
  Etiquette, 96.
  Expenses, 83, 101.
  Fire, 46, 66-69.
  Flies and mosquitoes, 98.
  Hammock, 64.
  Hitching-post, 64, 96.
  Independence, 12, 97.
  Ladies, 41, 93-95.
  Lamp and lantern, 61.
  Mattress, 63.
  Mosquito-bar, 98.
  Outfit, 10-13, 20-22.
  Shelters, 69-71, 96.
  Sleeping, 55, 62.
  Stoves, 39-43.
  Tents, 72-89.

# INDEX.

Camp-stoves, 39–43.
Candles and candlesticks, 61.
Captain for large party, 25–34.
Care of food, 47–49.
Cart, pulling a, 115.
Catching fish in nets, 101.
Cattle-paths the safest, 118.
Cellar, sunk barrel, 48.
Chafing the skin, 16, 52–54.
Cheap living, 102.
Children in camp, 94.
Chimneys, 67, 68.
Cholera morbus, 126.
Cloth for tent, 82.
    how to preserve, 83.
Clothes-line in tent, 61.
    on camp-ground, 64.
Clothing, 35–38.
    made early, 10.
    for mountain climbing, 58.
    at night, 19, 64.
Climbing mountains, 14, 57.
    with safety, 117.
Coffee better than alcohol, 55, 124.
    pot, 41, 45.
Cold weather, what to do in, 66.
    "taking cold," 118.
Collars to shirts, 35.
Compass points not known, 91.
Cooking, 44–47.
    utensils, 20, 42–46.
    stoves, 39–41.
Costiveness, 55.
Cover for wagon, 25.
Cunners, how skinned, 100.
    how caught in net, 101.
Daily tour of duty, 26–29.
Diary, how to keep, 107–112.
Diarrhœa, 126.
Dishes, 11.
    to be brought on table, 97.
Dish-cloths, 49.
Drawers, 36.
Drawing sketches advised, 109.
Drinking water, 51, 121.
    coffee and tea, 55, 124.
    oatmeal, 52.
    liquors, 55, 123.
Driving a wagon, 32, 34.
    a stake into ground, 96.
Drowning, to revive from, 126–128.
Dutch oven, 42.
Eat sparingly on return home, 105.
    before walking, 113.
Etiquette of camp, 96.
Exercise not good after meals, 50.
Expenses, 10, 15, 23, 26, 83.
    of trips to White Mts., 34.
    of a supposed trip, 101–105.
Farmers, how to treat, 56.

Fatigue, 54, 56, 122.
Fiddles of a tent, 82.
"Fighting cut" to hair, 11.
Fire, danger from, 68–70.
    kind of to cook upon, 46.
    for cold weather, 66, 69.
First day's march, 51, 52, 55.
Fish, how preserved, 48.
    how to skin, 100.
    to catch in nets, 101.
Fishermen's treatment of cloth, 84.
Flies and mosquitoes, 98.
    short hair no protection, 12.
    mosquito-bars, 99.
Fly for tent, 82.
Floor for tent, 60.
Food, 20.
    care of, 47–49.
    expense of, 102.
Footsoreness, 52–54.
    (*see* shoes), 36.
Frying, 44–46.
Frying-pan, tin plate, or canteen, 44.
    bring it on the table, 97.
Getting ready, 9–13.
Glycerine for sunburn, &c., 53.
Guy-lines of tent, 81.
Hair, how cut, 11.
Hammock, 64.
Handbarrow, 60.
Harness, 30, 32.
Hatchet, 20.
Haversack, how made, 18.
Hip-pantaloons, 37.
Hitching-post, 64, 96.
Horse and wagon for baggage, 25–34.
Horseback tour, 90.
Hotels to be avoided, 56, 105.
"How to do it," 113–116.
Hunger, none first day, 55.
    and fatigue, 122.
Hunter's camp, 69.
Hygienic notes, 117–129.
Independence in camp, 12, 97.
    in modes of travel, 115.
Insect in ear, 126.
Knapsack, 11, 16.
    the roll a substitute, 16–17.
Ladies need a stove, 41.
    climbing mountains, 58.
    as pedestrians, 93.
    outfits for, 94, 95.
    and children in camp, 94.
Lamp and lantern, 61.
Leggings for foot-travellers, 54.
Lime-water on tent-cloth, 84.
Liquors not needed, 55, 123.
Lobsters caught in net, 101.
Lost, whereabouts, and direction, 91.
Lumbermen's way to carry pork, 48.

# INDEX. 133

Lumbermen's way to cook beans, 46.
Map, study before travel, 92.
Management of party, 25-29, 33, 34.
Marching, 50-59.
    in army, 50.
    first day's troubles, 51.
    second day's fatigue, 54.
    how fast, 23, 50, 102, 114.
    hundred miles a week, 102.
    "How to do it," 113, 114.
Mark name on baggage, 10.
Mattress, 63.
Medicines, 55.
Mildew, how to prevent, 83.
Mosaic law, 65.
Mosquitoes and flies, 11, 98.
Mountain climbing, 14, 57.
    for ladies, 58.
Mutton tallow for chafing, &c., 53.
Nails in shoes, 37.
Net, mosquito, 98.
    to catch fish, 101.
Note-book, 10, 110.
Oatmeal in water, 52.
Offal to be buried, 65.
Oil of cedar and pennyroyal, 99.
    for sunburn, chafing, &c, 53.
    for harness and boots, 32.
Opodeldoc for mosquito-bites, 99.
Outfit, 10-13, 19-22, 102.
Overcoat not needed, 19.
    needed on mountains, 58.
Overloading, 15, 90, 102.
Packing a wagon, 26, 32.
    away tents, 89.
Pantaloons, 37.
    in stockings, 54.
Parents, advice to, 105.
Perspiration, nature of, 120.
Pillow carried by officer, 21.
Poisons, treatment for, 128.
Poles for tent, 60, 73, 79, 82.
    how made, 86.
Politeness, 56, 97.
Pork and beans baked, 47.
    how carried, 48.
Postal cards as stencil-plates, 10.
Potatoes for food, 103.
    candlesticks, 61.
Preparations, 9.
Privies, 65.
Public resorts to be avoided, 56, 105.
Racing with locomotives, 114.
Rations, 22, 102-104.
Recipes for cooking, 46-47.
Reckoning lost, 91.
Rests frequent advised, 50, 113, 114.
    should not be long, 50.
    at halts, 50, 56.
    to prevent sunstroke, 121.

Roll better than knapsack, 17.
Rotten trees dangerous, 60.
Route should be known, 9, 23, 92.
Rubber blanket, 16, 22, 58.
    for tents, 75.
    boots for dew, 95.
Sail-boat, 90, 118.
Salve for sunburn, chafing, &c., 53.
Screens of bushes, 60, 96.
Second day's march fatiguing, 54.
Shaving the head not advised, 11.
Shelters, 69-71, 96.
Shelter-tent, 17, 19, 70, 72-75.
    how to pitch, 70, 73-75.
    how made, 72-74.
    not good for ladies, 94.
    illustration of, 129.
Shirts instead of overcoat, 19.
    how made, 35.
    undershirts, 38.
Shoes, 36.
    slippers, 120.
Sickness: —
    Liability to, 14, 23, 55, 106.
    Remedies, 120, 121, 126.
    Insect in ear, 126.
    Cholera morbus, 126.
    Drowning, to restore from, 126-128.
    Poisons, treatment for, 128.
Sinks, 65.
Sketching advised, 109.
Skinning fish, 100.
Sleep on a hay-mow, 23.
    difficult first night, 54.
    for your comrades, 55.
    (*see* beds), 62.
    general advice about, 63, 64.
Slippers, 120.
Sluts for light, 62.
Smudge for mosquitoes, &c., 100.
Soap for footsoreness, &c., 53.
    tents, 83.
Socks, 37.
Sod-cloth of tents, 78, 81.
Soldier's weight of outfit, 15.
    German, 16.
    rule for drinking, 51.
    trousers in socks, 54.
    preventive for chafing, 54.
    mattress, 63.
    shelter-tents, 72.
    rations, 103.
Spade, uses of, 47, 65, 88.
Speed proper to walk, 23, 51, 102, 114.
Spirits not needed, 55.
Stake, how driven, 96.
Starvation, do not risk, 21.
Stays to tent, 84.
Stencil-plate of postal card, 11.
Stimulation, nature and effects, 123.

# INDEX.

Stockings, best kind on march, 37.
    pantaloons tucked into, 54.
    take off when wet, 120.
Stoves, &c., 11, 39-43.
    portable, 39-41.
    inside tent when cold, 66.
    top, 42.
Summer-houses, screens, &c., 96.
Sunburn, 53.
Sunstroke, 121.
Suspenders, 38.
Supplies for camping enumerated, 13.
Swimming, 118.
Table manners in camp, 96.
Taking cold, 118.
Tanning tent-cloth, 84.
Tea better than alcohol, 55, 124.
Tents, 72-89.
    best kind to use, 19, 88.
    made in wagon, 25.
    how to make "shelter," 72.
    how to make "A," 75.
    how to make "wall," 80.
    how to pitch "wall," 85.
    cloth for, 82.
    cloth, how preserved, 83, 89.
    fly, 82.
Tent-poles, whether to carry, 20.
    how made, 73, 79, 86.
    hand-barrow, 60.
Tent-pins, 20, 87.
Thirst, 51, 52, 121.
Tobacco, when to use, 124.
Tools, 25.
Training before journey, 12, 102.
Travelling acquaintances, 97.

Travelling afoot, 12, 14-34.
    horseback, 90.
    boating, 90, 118.
    expenses, 15, 23, 26, 34, 102.
    how fast, 23, 50, 102, 114.
    with hand-cart, 115.
Trench for offal, 65.
    around tent, 84.
    for fireplace, 67.
Trousers, 37-38.
Tub in boat, 91.
Ventilation, 64.
Wagon, general advice, 25, 31-33.
    made into tent, 25.
    man to walk behind, 34.
Walking, 50-59.
    how fast, 23, 50, 102, 114.
    at noon, 114.
    parties in White Mts., 34.
    one hundred miles, 102.
    eat before, 113.
Wall-tent, how made, &c., 80.
    to pitch quickly, 85.
Warm, how to keep, 66-70.
Water for drinking, 51.
    how to carry in pails, 68.
    none on mountains, 58.
Weekly supply for two men, 102.
Weight of outfit, 15, 21-23.
Wet and taking cold, 120.
    clothes, weight, 22.
Whims of soldiers, 21.
Woodman's camp, 69.
Woollen blanket, 19, 22.
    shirt, 19.
Yankee baker, 43.

www.ingramcontent.com/pod-product-compliance
Lightning Source LLC
Chambersburg PA
CBHW020104170426
43199CB00009B/386